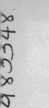

Going to

HOW YOU CAN COPE, REGROUP, AND

Plan B

START YOUR LIFE ON A NEW PATH

NANCY K. SCHLOSSBERG &

SUSAN PORTER ROBINSON

A FIRESIDE BOOK
PUBLISHED BY SIMON & SCHUSTER
New York London Toronto
Sydney Tokyo Singapore

F

FIRESIDE
Rockefeller Center
1230 Avenue of the Americas
New York, NY 10020

FIRESIDE and colophon are registered trademarks of Simon & Schuster Inc.

DESIGNED BY BARBARA MARKS

Manufactured in the United States of America

10 9 8 7 6 5 4 3 2 1

Library of Congress Cataloging-in-Publication Data

Schlossberg, Nancy K., date.
    Going to plan B : how you can cope, regroup, and start your life on
a new path / Nancy K. Schlossberg & Susan Porter Robinson.
        p.   cm.
    Includes bibliographical references and index.
        1. Disappointment.   2. Disappointment—Case studies.
3. Life change events.   4. Adjustment (Psychology)   I. Robinson,
Susan Porter   II. Title.
BF575.D57S35   1996
158'.1—dc20   95-41902
                                                           CIP

ISBN: 0-684-81149-9

Grateful acknowledgment is made to the following for permission to
reprint previously published material:
    From "Don't Act Your Age" by Carol Tavris. Copyright © 1989 by
Carol Tavris. Originally appeared in *American Health*.
    From *Nora* by Sandra Meagher.

For Susan J. Tolchin, whose friendship and
persistence helped make this book a reality,

and

Steve, Karen, and Mark,
my constant champions

—Nancy K. Schlossberg

For Jamie,
Malia, Melanie, and Nathan—
the best events of my life

—Susan Porter Robinson

Contents

ACKNOWLEDGMENTS   13
PREFACE   17

PART I. NOTHING HAPPENED:
EVERYTHING CHANGED   23

1. NON-EVENTS:
   A NEW NAME FOR HEARTBREAK?   25
   The Many Faces of Loss   28
      A Matter of Timing   28
      Surprises, Not Stages   31
      The Importance of Failure   32
   A Tale of Two Non-Events   33
   So What Did We Learn?   35

2. EVERYONE'S STORY   37
   Where Broken Dreams Reside   38
   The Stuff That Dreams Are Made Of   40
      Reluctant Chips Off the Old Block   42
      Chips Who Never Leave the Block   42
      Chips Who Only Thought They'd Left the Block   43
   Tracking Our Dreams: Triggers and Types   44

Gauging the Impact of Non-Events   45
 Hopeful or Hopeless   46
 Sudden or Gradual   47
 In or Out of Our Control   48
 Positive, Negative, or Neutral   49
Coping With Non-Events: The Dream-Reshaping Process   50
 Acknowledging   52
 Easing   52
 Refocusing   52
 Reshaping   53
Wrapping It Up   53

PART II: IDENTIFYING A NON-EVENT
IN THE VAST FIELD OF DREAMS   55

3. *LOVE AND FAMILY*   57
When Romantic Love Eludes Us   60
 In Search Of   62
 The Missing Mate   64
 Wondering What Might Have Been   65
 The Sexless Marriage   66
Such Good Friends   66
When Family Deals Us a Non-Event   68
 Family and Other Forms of Life   68
 The Future Deferred   69
 The Empty Cradle   70
 Miscarriage: The Silent Loss   73
 A Dream Too Late   74
 Infertility and Surprise Endings   75
 The Incomplete Family   76
 Bemoaning the Serpent's Tooth   78
 When Parents Don't Deliver   80
 The Sibling Non-Bond   80
 Gay and Lesbian Families   81

A Final Case in Point   82

Conclusion   84

4. THE DREAM OF SUCCESS   87

Career and Competence   89

Shifting Times in the Workplace: Transformed Assumptions   90

Moving In: When Success Eludes Us   92

    The Missing Laurel   93

    Hands That Never Rocked the Cradle   95

Moving Through: Even the Pope Plateaus   96

    Traitors in Their Midst   97

    An Inheritance Lost   98

    Reaching for the Snooze Button   99

    Hints of a Workplace Revolution   100

Moving Out: On the Road Again   101

Success and Intimacy: The Overlapping Dreams   103

    His World, Her World   104

    Sex-Role Bias Dies Hard   106

    Moving In, Out, Then Up: One Woman's Story   107

The Meanings of Our Success   109

    Right Guy, Wrong Path   109

5. SELF AND LEGACY   113

The Me Nobody Knows   114

    Our Imperfect Bodies   117

    Mind Over Matter   118

    That Elusive Inner Peace   120

    Our Spirits, Our Selves   122

    The Ideal Me, the Ideal I   123

Legacy—Our Once and Future Gift   125

    The Need to Transfer   126

    The Need to Matter   130

Culture and Politics: The Larger Legacies   133

Self and Legacy: A Final Glance   134

PART III: COPING AT LAST: THE DREAM-RESHAPING PROCESS   135

6. ACKNOWLEDGING THE LOST DREAM   137
   Public Versus Private Non-Events: Tell Us Where It Hurts   142
   Making Meaning   142
       Naming   144
       Telling Your Story   146
       Using Metaphors   148

7. EASING YOUR NON-EVENT STRESS   151
   Emotions as Signals   153
       Anger   155
       Anxiety   156
       Shame and Guilt   157
       Regret: Similar but Not Matching   159
       Sadness and Depression   160
       Apathy   160
       Envy   161
       Relief   161
       Hope   162
   Labels: Easing With Accuracy   163
       A View of Our Own   164
       Blame: Its Use and Abuse   166
   Good Grief: It Could Change Your Life   167
       Expressing the Emotions of Grief   170
       Non-Events: When Dreams Are Fulfilled!   170
   Other Non-Event Relief   171
       Seeking Support   171
       Journal Writing   173
       Faith   174
       Humor   176
       Stress-Reduction Techniques: A Potpourri   177
   In Praise of Way Stations   179

CONTENTS

8. *SHIFTING THE FOCUS TO HOPE*   181

Some Views of the Bridge   182

On the Road Again   182

Limbo   185

Finding a Place to Call Home   187

Non-Event Variety: One Lens Doesn't Fit All   189

Personal   189

Ripple   190

Resultant   192

Delayed   193

Refocusing, Reframing, and Other Optic Strategies   194

Letting Go of Expectations   194

Facing Your Illusions: A Double-Edged Sword   196

Reframing the Picture   198

Rites of Passage: Outward Signs of Inner Change   200

9. *RESHAPING THE DREAM*   205

Possible Dream Paths   207

Revisiting Hope   207

The Slow Road Home   209

A Thousand Possible Lives   211

Seeds of Transformation   212

Your Strategies: Conscious Coping   213

When hope abounds: Using problem-focused strategies   214

When hope is absent: Using emotion-focused strategies   215

Your Self: Dreaming the New and the Possible   216

Your Supports: Allies and Assets Along the Way   217

Your Situation: Grim, Great, or Somewhere in Between   218

Phoenix rising: A survivor's story   218

AFTERWORD: FROM HEARTACHE TO HOPE   223

NOTES   227

INDEX   231

Acknowledgments

This book has been four years in the making—during which time we listened, probed, read, and grappled with what finally became more testament than task for each of us. Though no one who's ever written a book would suggest, even in the glow of hindsight, that the process is totally satisfying, the sum of this venture has been greater than its parts for several reasons.

First, we were offered countless stories, the privileged confidences of adults who were anxious to be understood—many for the first time. For the gift of their trust, we will always be grateful. Second, in learning about others, we learned about ourselves, and our respondents had much to teach us about loss and subsequent gains. Third, we became the fortunate heirs of women and men whose research is cited throughout this book. We felt like weavers, winding their thoughts into a larger whole, watching their legacy enrich another loom.

We are grateful to the following friends, family, and mentors:

- To Margaret Zusky from Lexington Books, who first encouraged Nancy to write on non-events and later introduced us to our agent. Without Margaret, this book itself might well have been a non-event.
- To our agent, Anne Edelstein, that rare blend of compe-

tence and kindness who made the last leg of this journey so much more tolerable.

❦ To Sheila M. Curry, our editor at Simon & Schuster, who told us "I should be the editor for this book." And she was right.

❦ To Laureen Connelly Rowland, our final editor, who steered us through the remaining stages with enthusiasm and good humor.

❦ To those who helped with the research, including Janice Altman, Leah Steinberg, Robert Lissitz, Lisa Heiser, and Nancy Bruns.

❦ To Ilene Siegler, who first introduced Nancy to the concept and importance of non-events.

In our personal worlds, we are also grateful:

❦ To author and friend Susan Tolchin for her generous support and editing of the proposal when we truly needed both.

❦ To Betty Bowers, our veritable right hand, whose typing, rearranging, schlepping, and good cheer were unfailing from the beginning.

❦ To Stephen Sattler, who read, edited, listened, advised—and cared above all.

❦ To Celia Coates, psychotherapist and healer, whose wisdom informs so many of these pages.

❦ To Beverly Popek and Mark Griffin, whose lake house and generous caretaking spawned many a revision.

❦ To Sylvia Rosenfield, chair of the Counseling and Personnel Services Department at the University of Maryland at College Park, and Henry Spille, vice president at the American Council on Education. It is in their very natures to be supportive and they were—in ways they little imagine.

❦ To many other friends and colleagues who helped refine our thinking.

We also wish to thank Susan's three children, Malia, Melanie, and Nathan. For all the times you were quiet, helpful, and courteous when Mom was otherwise engaged, thanks, a lot.

Thanks also to Nancy's grown children, Karen and Mark, who provided good stories of their own as the book got under way. You've taught us that letting go isn't easy—even for women who write about it.

Finally, a special thanks to our husbands, Steve Schlossberg and Jamie Robinson. In this work, as always, you've each been teacher, anchor, helpmeet, and friend.

NANCY K. SCHLOSSBERG
SUSAN PORTER ROBINSON

Preface

The longest journey

Is the journey inwards.

—DAG HAMMARSKJOLD[1]

In his bestselling book *The Song of the Bird*, the late Jesuit author Anthony de Mello related a simple parable: One day a wise man was walking through the jungle. Suddenly, from a tree high above him, a vicious monkey hurled a coconut at the wise man's head. Bending down, the man picked up the coconut, drank its milk, ate its meat, and fashioned a bowl out of the coconut shell. Then he calmly walked on.[2]

This story illustrates responding to misfortune with the self-nurturing decision to extract the good from a situation. However, misfortune isn't always the result of something that happens to us; it is often the result of a lost or unfulfilled dream. When most of us imagine lost dreams, the losses are usually grand: losing a presidential election, failing as an actress, or forfeiting a musical or athletic career through some turn of fate.

But lost dreams can and do happen to everyone. Almost every one of us has had reasonable expectations for ourselves, our lives, or our loved ones that were not fulfilled despite our best efforts. Sometimes nothing happens—and therein lies the key to what we call non-events. Although little explored, non-events play a powerful role in shaping our lives.

In a culture and age when we're expected to "just do it," it's disconcerting when we just can't. Or as one attorney told us:

> *I hate people asking me "What's new?" It's as if my life is valued by its events, and yet all I talk about with my therapist are my disappointments, the clients that don't materialize, the cases never undertaken. That's what I care about. But the "public" me can*

only discuss the very opposite—the cases I do handle, the accomplishments I have made.

This book examines the role of non-events for adults and asks: What *are* non-events? How do they affect our lives, our roles, and our relationships? And most important, how do we cope with them?

Are non-events a new phenomenon, the product of an age of high hopes and great achievement? Hardly. Non-events have always been with us. Columbus did not sail around the world; Napoleon and Josephine were never married; and some of our greatest screen stars will never receive Oscars.

Non-events also appear in literature. In "The Beast in the Jungle," for example, Henry James describes a relationship that never developed romantically. In perhaps the most famous "non-event" play of all, *Waiting for Godot,* Samuel Beckett focuses on two vagabonds as they await the arrival of a man who never appears.[3] Godot, of course, has been ascribed a number of roles by literary critics—that of God, life, fate, failure, or savior. Regardless of the interpretation, the play is both comic and tragic, with an important lesson to be gleaned from this seemingly grim concept.

History and literary examples aside, however, the field of non-event research has been remarkably empty. Among the few studies that do allude to non-events are those of career counselor Janice Chiappone[4] and psychologist David Chiriboga,[5] who mention non-events as an important aspect of the adult years. But little is known about the range of non-events, about their long-term impact, and most especially about the strategies—effective and otherwise—that adults have used in confronting them.

The inquiry into non-events began when a research team at the University of Maryland at College Park collected accounts of non-events from over one hundred graduate students, training directors from business and industry, and returning students.[6] In doing so, they found that each of these adults had a sense of some failure that revolved around a range of non-events: relationships that did not materialize, careers that never developed, books that weren't published, or selves that never improved.

In the next stage of research, scenarios of typical non-events were developed. Sixty-two adult students—ages twenty-five to sixty—were asked to compare these non-event scenarios. Responses to the questionnaire then enabled the Maryland team to get a better understanding of the unique characteristics of non-events. They found that the adults' reactions to major disappointments depended on whether the events were seen as hopeful or hopeless, sudden or gradual, negative or positive, and in or out of their control.

In addition, we interviewed fifty retired volunteers aged fifty-five and over at the University of Maryland at College Park, and fifty others of all ages from many walks of life. We asked them all, "Do you think a study of lost dreams would be of use? If so, why?" The answers suggested that non-events are widespread (virtually every respondent described one), and almost all the respondents, regardless of age or sex, felt further exploration would be "extremely helpful." As one woman noted, "Lost dreams seriously impact your life and a study would bring a sense of realism to the idea and perhaps strategies for coping." Another respondent had felt isolated with his disappointment: "Knowing that others suffer over unmet expectations and that they often can't get over their thoughts about lost love, lost career, a lost self would help people feel not so alone."

We too have faced non-events and learned about reshaping our dreams. Between us, we have five children, all adopted when infertility threatened the dream of family. Between us, we've experienced a graduate degree unfinished, illness when we expected health, and various career plans that didn't develop. When our research for this book began, however, we didn't anticipate the overwhelming interest of almost everyone we approached about the subject.

If we are to believe Henry David Thoreau's lament that "most men [and women] lead lives of quiet desperation," then undoubtedly this low-grade despair derives from a disappointing life. Often, we've found, the source of this dissatisfaction is a non-event—an expectation that has gone unmet over time. More positively, though, adults who finally identify their non-events can find both relief and alternative paths.

This book then is not about failure, but about process—the process of discovery and the reclamation of a dream. The difficulty with non-events, of course, is that they are more challenging than events to define; they don't have the clear boundaries of events and closure is often more elusive. Part I, "Nothing Happened: Everything Changed," provides a basic understanding of non-events: that they occur in many areas of adult life, that they affect us in many ways, and that they touch the lives of virtually everyone.

Part II, "Identifying a Non-Event in the Vast Field of Dreams," lays the groundwork for the areas of our lives where happiness and heartache most readily occur. Part III, "Coping at Last: The Dream-Reshaping Process," describes the process for coping with non-events. The need for such a process became clear as we discovered how adults struggle—and not always successfully—to deal with life's disappointments. The strategies of this process are not linear, however, nor will every reader find them equally useful. Rather, imagine you're like a traveler who drives from Maine to California for the first time. You'll use a map along the way, but the recommended route will be revised as you encounter construction, inclement weather, and a dozen unforeseen changes. Still, the map is essential as you journey in a general direction. So too a reshaping process is useful as you leave behind your shattered dreams and head out to claim new ones.

The stories in this book are all true, although names and sometimes circumstances are altered to protect the privacy of the interviewees. Occasionally, the accounts are composites. As you will see, many of the stories are about loss and some are about survival. But ultimately, this is a book about hope. As you journey inward to examine your own loss and its promise, perhaps these pages will guide you to new dreams. We all need companions on the way.

Nothing

Happened:

Everything

Changed

1

Non-Events:
A New Name
for Heartbreak?

Dreams are necessary to life.

—ANAÏS NIN[1]

Most of us dream of someone to love, of creating a family, of succeeding in our work, or of making our portion of the world a safer and better place to be. When these dreams are broken, when expectations are unmet and plans go unrealized, lives can be shattered. These broken dreams, of course, are only part of a life's story. But they are largely untold and unexamined. *What if* there are no significant others to love? No babies to hold? No careers at which we excel? What if our dreams don't fit our own or others' expectations? Understanding these "non-events" can provide the opportunity to reevaluate our lost dreams and explore promising alternatives. And in doing so, we may find that we haven't lost a dream after all, but recaptured its very essence.

Just what *is* a "non-event"? A non-event is simply the event that *doesn't* happen. It is also the event that you reasonably expect will happen, and its absence can change your life. For example:

- ❦ I expected to go to a prestigious journalism school. I didn't get admitted. I accepted a marriage proposal because I felt that I needed support. I then began to take on the aspirations of my husband and I neglected myself.
- ❦ I always expected to be a parent. My wife had four miscarriages and she refuses to adopt. I am struggling with what to do now.
- ❦ I'm an editor at a fairly large publishing house. Though I'm hardworking and have good contacts, I never seem

to land a significant book. Nor am I ever promoted. After eight years, I expected to be much further along in my career than this.

❦ I always wanted to be a pilot. I trained as one in the military and gave twenty years of my life flying for the armed services. Now I'm "retired" at age forty-two. I thought I could fly for the major airlines, but they're inundated with applicants. The "minors," or commuter lines, pay slave wages. After months as a pilot for a commuter line and being separated from my family, it finally hit me: Being a commercial pilot just isn't going to happen.

❦ Year after year, my sorority entered me in our university beauty pageants. And year after year, I stood on the stage, nervously holding my stomach in, smiling for the judges, and hoping. And I never won, not once. I'm nearly seventy years old now, so it's been fifty years. But somehow I can still remember how it felt.

❦ You don't often read about "secondary infertility," but it's a fact. I gave birth to a beautiful little girl in my early thirties and imagined that she'd have a little brother or sister before too long. That second child never came. I know I'm lucky to have my daughter, but there are many women like me who didn't really want to stop with one child. People just assume they did.

❦ All through grade school, high school, and college, I took dance classes. First classical, then modern ballet. I lived to dance, in fact, and dreamed of joining a professional troupe when I graduated. That dream may seem naive, but every spare moment of my growing years was devoted to that dream. I give dance lessons part-time now, but I still think of what might have been—if I had had more talent, if someone had given me a chance, if, if, if . . .

Each of these people has experienced that sense of what-might-have-been, the earnest expectations that were not met, the dreams that somehow got lost along the way.

THE MANY FACES OF LOSS

Part of the challenge of dealing with these disappointments is that non-events are characterized by what they are not. Because they are generally hidden from view, non-events are not acknowledged, celebrated, or ritualized in any way. Yet their ability to gnaw at our insides—whether we are conscious of our lost dreams or not—often produces feelings of sadness, anxiety, or just a vague dissatisfaction with ourselves and our lives.

When we say that a non-event is the absence of an event that can be *reasonably* expected to occur, the key words are "absence" and "reasonably expected." The absence part is easy. Something does not happen. The "reasonably expected" aspect, however, initially caused a little confusion with some of our interviewees. True, we could all bemoan the Pulitzers and pageants not won, the master's and marathons not completed. But a non-event is more aligned with *probability* than with possibility. Johanna, our would-be beauty queen, was beautiful and had every reason to expect to win at least one of the many pageants she entered. Robert had twenty years of training and experience that should have qualified him for a pilot's job with a major airline. Only when an event is *likely* to occur, but doesn't, can we consider it a non-event.

A MATTER OF TIMING

In infancy, childhood, and even adolescence, behavior is controlled to a considerable extent by biological clocks. For example, we toddle, then walk as the result of physical maturation. In adulthood, however, as psychologist Bernice Neugarten suggests, behavior is controlled primarily by a social rather than a biological clock.[2] As a consequence, most of us have ideas about what constitutes appropriate behavior for people at particular ages. For in adulthood, excepting menopause and illness, we have few biological punctuation marks that denote the ending of old behaviors and the beginning of new ones.

In the past, most popular writers on adult development focused on age as the marker for change in our lives. Today, however, an increasing number of professionals realize that transitions are more relevant than chronological age. On the positive side, we are being forced to reevaluate our social clocks and realize that age need not deter us from new goals. On the negative side, it is frightening to abandon the old scripts that "told" us what to do and when.

Yet, as we saw, we suffer needlessly when we judge ourselves and our lives by outdated standards. Many of the people we interviewed still clung to these old scripts and consequently felt "off-time." They believed that the events they expected *should* have occurred and that they themselves were woefully behind. But as we begin to see, for example, that first-time grandmothers can range in age from forty to eighty, we realize that there is no "right" age for that transition. Similarly, first-time parents may range in age from fifteen to over fifty.

This social fluctuation can be distressing, of course, as Neugarten observed:

> *Major stresses are caused by events that upset the sequence and rhythm of the life cycle—as when death of a parent comes in childhood rather than in middle age; when marriage does not come at its desired or appropriate time; when the birth of a child is too early or too late; when occupational achievement is delayed; when the empty nest, grandparenthood, retirement, major illness, or widowhood occur off-time. In this sense, then, a psychology of the life cycle is not a psychology of crisis behavior so much as it is a psychology of timing.*[3]

Understanding this psychology is central to the concept of non-events. We perceive ourselves as experiencing a non-event based on our social clocks, which in turn are often tied to cultural expectations. In fact, a non-event may be merely a delayed event. Consider Frank, who lamented: "My children are at the right age to be excelling in their careers, but they haven't even decided what those careers will be. I see this as a terrible loss." He did not see that his children might still have satisfying careers, and that today this apparent loss may simply be a delayed event—delayed in terms of Frank's own social clock. Changing his perspective could help him avoid pressuring his children the way Frank had been pressured by his own father.

The fact is that most adults do have expectations, internalized since childhood, about when they can reasonably expect certain major life events to occur. Maria cried the night before her twenty-seventh birthday. "I don't give a damn about a career. I want a baby and a family. It has not happened and I am beginning to believe it is never going to happen. I don't want to celebrate my birthday." For several reasons, Maria decided that her timetable had not been met. Since she is Hispanic, with a cultural heritage that is very family-oriented, Maria's non-event was a result of societal expectations as well as of her own individual assumptions about the way to live a life. Maria's personal sense of timing triggered a feeling of great loss as she faced this non-event. Ironically, to thousands of other women just beginning their careers, Maria's family-less situation could make pursuing a career much easier.

While cultural norms may shape our expectations, our circle of friends provides another profound influence. Cynthia related an experience with her thirty-three-year-old son: "Mark and I visited a friend who had recently given birth to her second child. We had a wonderful afternoon playing with the three-year-old, holding the baby, and admiring the mother, who was nurturing and enjoying her children. Though the new mother, Becky, told us she planned to return to work eventually, it was clear she relished her role as mother and caregiver. I left thinking what a splendid time we'd all had.

"Two nights later, however, Mark called me sounding upset. He had just broken up with his second partner in a year and he still is unclear about his career plans. Somehow, being with Becky that afternoon had triggered Mark's realization that he was 'nowhere,' that he had neither a relationship nor a meaningful career."

Clearly, our sense of timing is affected by those around us. A romantic breakup is difficult any time, but if Mark had been surrounded by other single friends the issue of timing would have been less painful. We need to consider, then, how much of our distress is caused by the lives and expectations of others.

SURPRISES, NOT STAGES

Age-related "stages" are no longer appropriate for adults. Significant transitions can happen—or fail to happen—at any time in adulthood, a belief echoed in the lament of social psychologist Carol Tavris.

> I survived Gesell's stages only to find myself, as a college student . . . assigned to read Erik Erikson's theory of the eight stages of man. . . . It turned out . . . that Erikson meant the ages of "man" literally. . . . We female students all protested that our stages were out of order. . . . [Then] in the 1970s, stage theory struck again with an eruption of popular books. . . . By this time I was really annoyed. I wasn't having any of my crises in the right order. I hadn't married when I was supposed to . . . leaving my job created an identity crisis at 32, far too late. I had only to look around to realize I was not alone. All sorts of social changes were detonating around me. Women who had been homebodies for 35 years were running off to start businesses, much to the annoyance of their husbands, who were quitting their businesses to take lute lessons. . . . People who expected to marry didn't. Women who

expected never to work were working. Men who expected never to care about babies were cooing over their own. Expectations were out the window altogether.[4]

Similarly, Mary Catherine Bateson observed in her book *Composing a Life* that life isn't linear, but rather fluid and even disjointed:

> *The model of an ordinary successful life that is held up for young people is one of early decision and commitment, often to an educational preparation that launches a single rising trajectory. . . . Many of society's casualties are men and women who assumed they had chosen a path in life and found that it disappeared in the underbrush.*[5]

Bateson captures the anguish of many people who feel they have not quite measured up. Bateson's book also underscores the need to rethink our definitions of life success. Theories of stages and continuity are too tidy, and irregularity and fluidity in our lives have become the norm.

THE IMPORTANCE OF FAILURE

Some time ago, we heard ten women who received Woman of Distinction awards describe their dreams and the paths they took to achieve them. Only one of the women addressed her personal disappointments and failures, implying that the plans that had gone awry were just as essential as her successes on the road to achievement. With her own light touch yet painful honesty, Erma Bombeck once described the same phenomenon:

> *I have several reactions when I hear people introduce me as a speaker. Sometimes the accolades are so glowing that I don't even recognize myself. I figure Mother Teresa just flew in to give the*

invocation. Other times I feel like bolting while I'm still ahead. But most of the time I feel as though the only decent thing I can do to justify such a tribute is to die. . . . I would like to propose a new wrinkle to introductions. Instead of listing a speaker's successes, why not list the failures? . . . [For example] born average, our guest tonight never rose above it. . . . Her first and last comedy album . . . raced to oblivion. . . . She has written numerous plays no one ever heard of because they never made it to the stage. . . . She has never won a Pulitzer Prize . . . never been invited to the White House for dinner . . . and has never been interviewed by Barbara Walters. . . .

Failing is what most of us do. We do that a lot more than we succeed. . . . So, if the speaker is such a loser, then what's the point of all those people listening to what she has to say? Because despite all the disappointments and the failures, she's still managed to go on breathing and put them aside.[6]

Not that we should solicit failure, of course. We just need to realize that our lives are shaped by innumerable forces, including successes *and* failures. And non-events are invariably among them.

A TALE OF TWO NON-EVENTS

Sometimes our non-events are self-evident, and an individual may move more obviously from despair to hope when the essence of a lost dream is reclaimed. At age thirty-plus, Madeleine found that her inability to conceive was a crushing non-event. Later, the adoption process seemed agonizingly slow. Over the course of the next eleven years, she adopted three children. Slowly, her friends' pregnancies lost their sting, and the childraising years were under way. Finally it hit Madeleine that, in her case, only a non-event could have made her particular family possible. Madeleine's experience, and many like hers, illustrates that a dream you may think you have lost could well lead to another that is far more wonderful—for you.

Madeleine's story is also an example of this essential change of heart. Initially, Madeleine had desperately wanted to have children. Like most would-be mothers, she equated getting pregnant with having a child, and when conception wasn't possible, she experienced a profound despair. Fortunately, she soon examined her deepest desires and realized that, while she *had* wanted to bear a child, having and raising a child was what she longed for most. At that point, Madeleine began to see herself in a new way, not as the mother of a biological child, but as the mother of a child—period. Years later, Madeleine reported her internal transitions to us in this way: "Because I had always wanted to be a mother and because I'd never imagined that I wouldn't be wearing maternity clothes or nursing my children, at first I couldn't see a way out of my despair. I saw myself as a walking biological failure. It was only when I began to see myself as a woman with options that my life began to change."

Unlike Madeleine, many adults may not perceive their own non-events and find themselves leading event*ful* lives that mask vague feelings of anxiety or disappointment. At first, Seth reported that he had no non-events. "My life is filled with events, with major happenings," he told us. We wondered at the time if perhaps non-events aren't as universal as we had thought. But soon Seth recounted a relationship with his father, who was, in his words, a "walking non-event."

At forty, Seth is married, the father of two small children, and the owner of a successful consulting firm. His life, not surprisingly, is filled with deadlines, budget balancing, hiring, firing, marketing, and the challenge of orchestrating all this with the demands of family. Yet Seth has a problem with a parent who himself never achieved what he expected in his life. It seems that Seth's father had moved from job to job over the years, never quite able to make a living, and finally, when he was fifty, quit working altogether. At that point, Seth's mother took over the support of the family. While this lifelong problem is distressing for the father himself, Seth and his family also continue to feel the effects of this despair. Today the father lives through his children's achievements and places enormous pressure on them to do better. Because he is so self-critical, this controlling behavior and criticism of his children have become an emotional burden for the family.

Seth eventually told us that his father's series of non-events had affected him more profoundly than he cared to admit. He is unhappy with his own responses to his father—emotions that range from intense anger to sadness to feeling protective of his children against their grandfather's tirades. But Seth also understands that he can't change his father and that he needs to lower his expectations and set limits with this difficult parent.

Seth's situation, of course, illustrates the fact that a non-event need not be your own unfulfilled dream to be significant. If you are not in the midst of a non-event yourself, you may well be in a relationship with someone who feels the pain of something that hasn't happened. Naturally, when people close to you are living out lives of broken dreams, their loss can affect your relationship with them and even your own view of life.

So What Did We Learn?

Through the initial research on non-events and our subsequent interviews, we intended to move beyond an inventory of dashed hopes and griefs and to discover what they have to teach us all. And in the process, we learned that:

- ❦ Almost everyone responds to the notion of non-events.
- ❦ The impact of non-events is strongly related to timing.
- ❦ People are eager to share their experience of non-events and frequently have a pressing need to do so.

❦ Non-events are deeply felt, and acknowledging them can bring relief (a good start, but certainly not enough).

❦ Identifying non-events can lead to a richer understanding of the adult years.

❦ Adults can cope creatively with life's non-events, but too frequently they don't know how.

❦ What seems like a non-event to one person (for example, infertility) might not be defined that way by someone else.

❦ Shattered dreams need not shatter lives. In fact, just the opposite can be true.

As a final note to this chapter, we should add our beliefs about psychotherapy. We believe that therapy or counseling can be a valuable tool for healing the pain of a non-event, and that no book is a substitute for a good therapeutic relationship. But, whether or not you choose to engage in therapy over a lost dream, whether you look to a book, a friend, or some Higher Power, the healing begins when you discover your non-event, grieve for its loss, ease the accompanying distress, refocus your thinking, and reshape your dreams and self-perceptions. But give up on your dreams? Let them dry up, wither, even die? Never.

We are born to dream.

2

Everyone's Story

At (fourteen) . . . you believe that if God were to make you a millionaire and an idol whose views on the world were eagerly sought by millions, that it would be no more than what you deserved.

—GARRISON KEILLOR[1]

hough many adults modify the egocentric fervor expressed by Garrison Keillor, a fourteen-year-old still lurks in most of us. We know that dreamer from our own experience, and we have heard repeatedly from the men and women whose stories are part of this book that adults too "dream big." As a consequence, most adults have also experienced broken dreams, some even born of the tentative longings of adolescence. But each person is different, each broken dream unique.

For many of us, the vague dissatisfaction we feel around a non-event is just that—vague. In fact, the aspirations of the human heart are so varied and complex that we need a framework to help us consider them. Thus non-events can be best understood if we examine:

- ❦ Where broken dreams reside.
- ❦ The stuff that dreams are made of.
- ❦ Tracking our dreams: triggers and types.
- ❦ Gauging the impact of non-events.
- ❦ Coping with non-events: the dream-reshaping process.

WHERE BROKEN DREAMS RESIDE

We found that non-events generally are related to the following issues: relationships that don't materialize; family problems; career anxieties; missed educational opportunities; issues related to our emotional, physical, intellectual, and spiritual selves; and the fear that our life is without lasting meaning.

Simplifying these areas still further, adults both dream and give shape to life plans that center on love, family, success, self, and legacy. Though we recognize that life is not tidy—for example, what starts out as a dream about career and success can spill over to family and self—we decided to discuss these dreams separately as a way to better understand their roles in our lives.

Psychologist Erik Erikson also explored these dreams in his groundbreaking theory of human development, which is so comprehensive it has provided the basis for a wealth of subsequent research.

Essentially, Erikson divides the life span into eight stages from infancy to old age. Each stage of life represents a new challenge for the individual and, in effect, a struggle between two conflicting issues. If the conflict of values for each of these ages is resolved positively, an individual will have hope, will, purpose, competence, fidelity, love, care, and wisdom. The earliest example of this can be found in infancy when a baby struggles (unconsciously, of course) with *basic trust of others* versus *mistrust*. If this conflict is resolved positively through a nurturing environment, a basic human strength will emerge. Erikson identifies this strength as *hope* that the world is a safe place to be. This strength in turn provides the foundation for all subsequent relationships.[2]

In recent years Erikson's work has come under attack for seeming to be too "male" and too linear. Psychologist Carol Gilligan,[3] for example, challenges Erikson's model as focusing only on men's march through a life of upward mobility. She is not alone in noting that "separation" (typically a more "masculine" virtue) has always been touted as a sign of maturity when, in fact, more recent research holds that "interdependence" (once held to be a "feminine" virtue) is a greater sign of maturity. However, while agreeing with Gilligan and others in principle, we believe that Erikson has identified the critical underlying concerns of both men and women—the need to hope, the push for purpose, the concern over competence, the striving for fidelity, love, care, and the potential attainment of wisdom.

It is also true that Erikson diagrams his work in a linear fashion, but at the same time, he proposes that people revisit each major issue as life unfolds. We too view these issues as recurring throughout life—somewhat like overlapping circles.

Using Erikson's schema, then, *relationship* non-events can be related to the issues of trust, fidelity, and love; *career* and education non-events to competence and purpose; *family* and *legacy* non-events to care and wisdom—and *self* non-events to all of the above.

THE STUFF THAT DREAMS ARE MADE OF

Although many of our issues are universal, some of those dreams are ours alone: private longings that gradually enter our consciousness as we get older. Other desires come from societal expectations—that we will love the opposite sex; that we will marry; that we will procreate; that we will create a wonderful home or be stunning successes in our careers or both.

Who determines what your dream will be? Perhaps best loved and remembered for the gifts he gave us surrounding myth, Joseph Campbell encouraged us to follow *our* "bliss"—not that of individuals around us. But each society has a strong set of myths, which tend to lay the groundwork for what that bliss will be.[4] If a myth is defined as an "unproved collective belief that is accepted uncritically and is used to justify a social institution," chances are that our dreams will be drawn from at least one, if not several, of our society's myths.

Let's take an example from women's lives. In the recent past, it was believed that a woman should put a man at the center of her life, with her own desires clearly in second place. Author Carolyn Heilbrun labeled these women "unambiguous."[5] That is, there was no doubt or ambiguity about who held center stage in the family, and any dreams to the contrary were usually squelched early on. For most of these women, not pursuing a career would not have constituted a societal non-event. Rather, it would have been the exceptional woman who did wish to have a career, and her failure to do so would have "merely" been an individual non-event.

For many women today, of course, not pursuing a career goal can become a non-event that is both individual *and* societal. At thirty-six, Pilar was a gifted music teacher and the mother of two children. When she became pregnant with her third child, however, her career began to falter. Finally, when her maternity leave expired, Pilar discovered that her school principal had replaced her. Though this was an ethically suspect move, the principal worked within the letter of the law to ease Pilar out and to hire a younger, less experienced woman. In a matter of months, Pilar had gone from being an employed mother of two to being an unemployed mother of three. Of course, most women in years past would have been content with the very demanding role of full-time mother. However, because of the tremendous influx of women into the workforce, "norms" have shifted and altered women's expectations. Part of Pilar's dilemma was a lack of clear choice—in either conceiving a third child or losing her job at the school. But, she explained, the blow went far beyond personal choice and diminished income. Pilar's expectations for herself were that she would be a mother *and* a musician. Further, she would have a successful career, as all her friends and older sisters did. The very hardest part, she confided, was feeling "diminished in the eyes of my family and colleagues. I love my baby and a career is actually unthinkable at the moment. But it's hard to be at home after the heady feelings of career success. Plus, women at my educational level today are somehow expected to work."

Why bother with a distinction between societal and individual non-events? Because it is important to understand whether your non-event is significant to you or the pressure to realize a dream is coming from elsewhere. You will cope differently with non-events that spring from dreams that are your own.

As we see from the examples above, many of our expectations come from the world around us. Sex roles in particular have societal roots, as does the physical appearance of each sex. For those of us who long for the Rubenesque age, the reality is that we're living in an era that values the flawless and the lean. Or is your non-event not being able to buy a house? Not amassing a sizable bank account? Or not raising children who are college-bound? Those expectations too may well be more society's than your own.

RELUCTANT CHIPS OFF THE OLD BLOCK

Parental pressure is not uncommon in the area of non-events. Too frequently adult children are disappointed in lost dreams that were never theirs to begin with. Adrienne was turned down by a modeling agency when she was twenty-six. Suddenly, she lamented, she felt "old, ugly, and used up." At that point, Adrienne turned her attention to office work and was promoted within eight months. Still disappointed in herself, however, she imagined that she'd let her mother down. Fortunately, a colleague set her straight: "Is modeling really the kind of life you want for yourself—to be washed up at twenty-six, to value yourself for externals and not for your mind or creativity?" The frank discussion that ensued helped Adrienne to see that the dream had really been her mother's, not her own.

CHIPS WHO NEVER LEAVE THE BLOCK

In our society, at least among certain groups, young people are expected to move out of their parental home in their early twenties. That transition may occur when they go off to college or get their first "real" jobs. Today, however, because of economic pressures, a growing number of young people are returning to the nest. The ensuing non-event for parents—not having an empty nest—can be deeply upsetting because many of them long for that time when their lives are once again their own. Non-events that are both societal *and* individual can be the most painful of all. As one respondent, Edna, explained: "All of my friends' children have graduated from college and now have their own apartments and promising new jobs. I hate feeling ashamed that my son is still living at home, but I'm embarrassed when my friends talk about their children's touching attempts at decorating their new digs. I wish my son would make some touching attempts at decorating anything besides our kitchen with his dirty dishes. Add to this the fact that my husband and I feel we finally deserve our privacy. We worked hard to raise our three sons. It should be our turn now." Similarly, children who don't or can't leave home in early adulthood may also experience frustration. Sometimes their anger is turned outward—however irrationally—at their parents. Other times, these adult children are mortified that they can't "make it" on their own.

CHIPS WHO ONLY THOUGHT THEY'D LEFT THE BLOCK

More often than not, we leave the homes of our childhood and our children eventually leave ours. But a deeper, more essential leavetaking may never take place. Emotional separation is essential to maturation and even to realizing our own dreams.

Krista is a case in point. At sixty, this attractive woman has a lot to be proud of. She is a wife, mother, grandmother, and successful psychotherapist. And while each role has brought its attendant satisfactions, Krista feels a persistant restlessness.

To begin with, Krista grew up in a family that believed in unusually strong social commitment. She, in fact, holds those beliefs herself and has dreamed of starting an inner-city school, a goal that seems unlikely now. In one sense, this dream might be said to be individual, because it is certainly unique. However, the foundations for her dream were established within the "society" of her family. Perhaps Krista has separated in the healthiest sense, but the dream of a broader social commitment remains with her to this day and it nags her with surprising frequency.

Researchers claim that societal *events* and transitions are easier to deal with than individual ones because they can be anticipated and planned for. But this very fact can make societal *non*-events more difficult to deal with. Because these expectations have been held for so long, the impact can be painful when they do not occur.

TRACKING OUR DREAMS: TRIGGERS AND TYPES

Whether our thwarted goals are societal or individual, how do we know we are experiencing a non-event? Usually there is some kind of *trigger* that stimulates that awareness and reminds us that something is not happening.

Sometimes triggers are *external* reminders, as when a close friend publishes a book (and your manuscript has been turned down repeatedly). Or you're asked the invasive and all-too-familiar question: "When do you two plan to have children?" But sometimes a trigger is more subtle. Perhaps you hear that a distant relative is pregnant or a magazine opens to an article on maternity leave. These *internal* reminders, which are less obvious and personal, indicate that something just isn't happening.

Kevin worked hard during his first three years at a midsize company, unaware that his performance was not particularly valued by his superiors. When a position came open for which Kevin was well qualified, a less-experienced colleague was promoted and he was not. Naturally, with the colleague's second promotion, Kevin really began to feel the impact of his non-event. Kevin's trigger to realize his non-event was an external one.

Non-events are triggered in a number of ways. But triggers are only part of the non-event story. We can understand them more fully by differentiating four different types. Some non-events clearly happen to us as individuals; others ripple from someone else; still others are the result of another event; and some are merely delayed events. These distinctions provide an important way to think about non-events because they help us rethink our goals. At the same time, as we cite examples from many lives throughout this book, it's important to restate: What looms as a lost dream for one person is not necessarily one for another.

GAUGING THE IMPACT OF NON-EVENTS

"Fifty years later and I can still remember how it felt." That's what a would-be campus beauty queen told us, thereby providing a clear idea of how a non-event, never winning a pageant, had stayed with her over time. Did this loss change her roles during her college years? Later in life? Did it change her relationships? Her routines or assumptions about herself? The answers to these questions can measure the impact of a non-event.

A particular non-event may change an individual's role. For example, a woman who doesn't get promoted may suddenly find that a former colleague has become her supervisor. Not only did she not get the job, but her former role has actually changed from colleague to subordinate. Non-events may also affect us with changes in our daily routines. "I will never be able to have a baby. I will, therefore, go to school full-time." "I expected to retire but we cannot afford it, so my daily routines will not alter as expected." These changes can also include a new way of self-assessment—a change in assumptions: "I see myself as healthy and not dying as predicted."

In a sense, to qualify as a non-event, a non-event must change your life, but not all non-events change your life in the same way. Joel told us recently: "I have two children and I always expected that they would grow up, have careers, get married, and, of course, be close to me. After my wife and I got divorced, our daughter stopped speaking to me. She is twenty-nine and we haven't seen each other for ten years. I send her birthday and Christmas cards and wrote her a note when the dog died. She never writes or calls. My son has been hospitalized twice for mental illness. I also have lost contact with my siblings, another disappointment. When I think of all my losses, all my *non-events*, none compares with a child's poor mental health. Fortunately, this son is doing beautifully now . . . but these lost dreams all have had an impact on my life."

The effects of non-events vary and can be measured by whether they are seen as:

- Hopeful or hopeless.
- Sudden or gradual.
- In or out of our control.
- Positive, negative, or neutral.

HOPEFUL OR HOPELESS

The most crucial way in which non-events differ is in the degree of hope surrounding the threatened dream. Andrew recounted a health non-event that at first seemed hopeless. "I was diagnosed with scleroderma of the esophagus almost two years ago. It is a rare disease that is incurable and is fatal in most cases. A couple of months ago, I was told that I do not have the disease. My entire life had revolved around my illness. I needed to adjust to the new diagnosis and create goals suited to a healthy person."

When Andrew's diagnosis occurred, he lost all hope of living for very long. He changed his life, giving up his career to take a less demanding job. He also cut back on his relationships and became somewhat of a recluse. His family and few close friends tried to mobilize him to get out and socialize, but Andrew remained depressed and withdrawn. When it turned out that he did not have the disease, he was dismayed, then angry for all he had been put through needlessly. Within several weeks, however, Andrew began to feel hopeful that he could put together a life and feel some joy in living.

Non-events that have little hope attached to them are going to be perceived and reacted to very differently than more "hopeful" non-events. In one of the research studies, the issues of infertility, not having grandchildren, and rejection from a professional school were seen as the most hopeless.[6] Absence of marriage, surprisingly, was not seen as hopeless. It seems that many felt there was always the chance of meeting the partner of their dreams!

SUDDEN OR GRADUAL

As we indicated earlier in the section on timing, non-event triggers can be sudden, like a letter of rejection or a medical diagnosis. Or they can be more gradual, like the slow dawning of the realization that you will never permanently lose weight.

Career- or education-related non-events can be especially stressful. The rejection letter from a university arrives, the job is given to someone else, or the boss delivers the dreaded pink slip when there's a layoff. Because they are harder to anticipate, sudden non-events can be more difficult to handle and all but impossible to rehearse for.

After six years at a successful advertising agency, William, a forty-five-year-old executive, was called in with several other colleagues to learn about the company's reorganization. The severance pay would be generous, the benefits would continue for another six months, but the message was clear and swift: William would be out of a job in three weeks. In his case, there had been little indication beyond mild concern that business was not increasing. Still, the company had its excellent reputation and a stable of solid clients. What William and his coworkers hadn't anticipated, however, was that a decline in advertising in the early nineties signaled a downsizing in numerous industries.

Gradual non-events may be easier to take because we have time to get used to an idea. Perhaps the monthly reminder that a baby is not on the way is a major disappointment, but it is not as final as a letter that says "no." With gradual non-events, there's time to rehearse what life might be like if the expected doesn't occur. And that rehearsal is often vital to moving on. For years, Lynnette had tried to conceive a child, and by her early forties she had explored almost every medical avenue to make that happen. With each birthday, however, she began to let go of the dream, until finally she decided "enough of the grieving. My husband and I are wasting precious years of our lives, not to mention financial resources, in striving for a dream that will never be fulfilled—at least not biologically." Today Lynette volunteers at a local family shelter, tutoring school-age children and deriving great satisfaction from the youngsters she has helped. She also has thrown herself into her career more heartily and begun a considerable landscaping project. "It was a sad dress rehearsal for me each month," Lynnette explained, "but I slowly began to imagine a life without children of my own. I can't believe I'm finally saying this, but . . . I think I'm content at last."

IN OR OUT OF OUR CONTROL

Often we perceive non-events as out of our control. It is true that some non-events, such as infertility or not having grandchildren, are not in our power to change. Others, such as not getting promoted and even not getting married, actually can be.

A great deal of research demonstrates that control is crucial to mental health, and that need to feel in control is ingrained in our psyches from infancy on. We, however, need to remember that there are two aspects of control. We may not have a lot of control over some external events or non-events in our lives, but we do have significant power over our *reactions* to them. That is, a rejection from graduate school may be out of our hands, but we can control how we deal with the rejection and how we think about ourselves when the fateful letter arrives signifying that we might not be pursuing our dreamed-of career.

POSITIVE, NEGATIVE, OR NEUTRAL

The issue of controlling our responses has been addressed by psychologists Richard Lazarus and Susan Folkman, who highlight the importance of how we appraise or evaluate our transitions.[7] Do we perceive them to be positive, negative, or neutral? Most of the non-events we have uncovered are seen as losses. However, there are others that can be seen as positive. Most obvious, among those we've discussed so far, is the misdiagnosis of Andrew's fatal disease. There are also more subtle positive non-events, such as not getting our dream house in a neighborhood that, as it turns out, is scheduled for rezoning, or not getting a job we thought we wanted, only to discover the boss would have been a tyrant.

Andrew J. DuBrim, a corporate psychologist, cautions against holding on to dreams that may not be in our best interest. He writes:

> In the business world today, people tend to be judged—and to judge themselves—by how quickly they move up. Promotions are the barometer of progress and success. To stay at the same level— no matter how well you perform—is seen by many as failure.

> In fact, many people are better off without promotions The wrong promotion might undermine your family life . . . steal the satisfaction that comes from doing work you love . . . and ruin your career. Before accepting a higher position, consider whether you want it—and need it.[8]

Daydreaming helps us rehearse for future events *and* non-events to see how we would cope in any arena. Some women, in fact, mentally rehearse for widowhood, since that is a common occurrence for older women. But beware of over-rehearsing! Now sixty-four, Jan had been fearful for years that her husband would die of a heart attack. She had good reason. He had had several major heart attacks already and was ten years older than she. After forty years of marriage, however, she realized her most feared event—the death of her husband—had not occurred and that she couldn't reclaim those lost years of worry. We could all learn from Jan's experience of fretting unnecessarily and wasting time in the process.

Non-events, of course, are only positive if we perceive them that way. Hannah didn't get a higher-paying position she had wanted. As it turned out, the job would have been tedious and would not have been well suited to her talents. Three years later, Hannah has another job, which pays equally well and for which she is better equipped. Fortunately for her, a colleague stopped by her office the day she was turned down for the first promotion. "Congratulations," she told Hannah. "You didn't get the job. And by that I mean, you would have hated it!" This kind remark made all the difference in Hannah's perception of her loss, and this particular non-event was soon forgotten.

We've also had friends in the throes of illness, job demands, and family problems tell us they were actually longing for a non-event, sudden or otherwise: the precancerous polyp that doesn't develop into a malignancy, the difficult child who doesn't become the intolerable teen, the crisis at work that doesn't occur. Expressions like "Don't borrow trouble" and "Sufficient unto the day are the evils thereof" have their own collective wisdom, and non-events like these are blessings indeed.

COPING WITH NON-EVENTS:
THE DREAM-RESHAPING PROCESS

Adults are often at a loss when coping with non-events, and they like the notion of a process that will give their future shape. Holly complained as she struggled with forced retirement, "I think coping with a lost dream is harder because it's usually a hidden loss for which you don't rehearse." Rehearsal, however, is an essential coping strategy that eases the way into the future, enabling us to anticipate what's in store. What will I do the first day the baby comes home from the hospital? How will I dress those first days after retirement? Where will I go the day I leave my partner? These questions help a person to plan and make provisions for the next transition. On the other hand, since many non-events are sudden and unexpected, they are rarely rehearsed; in fact, there is seldom opportunity to plan for non-events. This factor alone makes coping with such losses different and difficult.

John, at least by his reckoning, is in the midst of several seeming "failures," but he is unable to move on. Looking at John's circumstances, you would see only success. His picture was in *Forbes*; his latest play was reviewed in *The New Yorker*. Yet secretly he is depressed. To begin with, John had expected that this play would be a blockbuster. It wasn't. John had also planned to make the rounds of the morning talk shows. He didn't. Rather than being thrilled with the spectacular success he has achieved, John is suffering because of what hasn't happened. It seems he never imagined, much less rehearsed, a life outside the limelight.

How might Holly, John, and each of us reshape our expectations and move beyond heartache? As with any process—cooking, cleaning, even surgery—not all people will reshape their dreams in the same order, nor should they. But, in general, we've discovered that a successful journey from loss to hope begins with acknowledging the lost dream, travels through a time of easing the discomfort, eventually turns to refocusing our thinking and thereby our lives, and ultimately enables us to reshape our dreams and move on.

As we examined these four components of the process—acknowledging, easing, refocusing, and reshaping—we selected strategies that might help with each. These strategies are not exhaustive, nor is the process a linear one. But most people experiencing a lost dream will probably find some of the processes and strategies (see table) useful.

THE DREAM-RESHAPING PROCESS

Acknowledging	Easing	Refocusing	Reshaping
Naming the non-event	Labeling emotional reactions	Letting go	Stocktaking
Telling a story	Grieving	Facing illusion	Regaining control
Using metaphors	Seeking support	Reframing	Imagining possible selves
Others	Journal writing	Developing rituals and rites of passage	Others
	Stress-reduction strategies	Others	
	Faith, humor		
	Others		

ACKNOWLEDGING

We can't deal effectively with a non-event until we "discover" it and give it a name. This has the twin benefit of diluting the power of a non-event and helping us take control of the situation. Strategies that uncover non-events so we can better manage them include *naming* and *labeling, telling a story,* and *using a metaphor.*

EASING

Often we need help in easing the distress that may come from the loss of a dream. Some alternatives that can help ease the way are *identifying the emotion resulting from the non-event, grieving, seeking support, journal writing, stress-reduction strategies, faith,* and *humor.*

REFOCUSING

Then we begin to "refocus"—to let go of old expectations and reframe our non-events. People often have difficulty leaving earlier images of themselves and their dreams in order to move on to new ones. *Letting go, facing illusions, reframing the picture,* and *developing rituals* and *rites of passage* are some refocusing strategies.

RESHAPING

Finally, we reshape our futures by identifying new dreams or fresh visions. This last part of the process includes *stocktaking, regaining control,* and *imagining a new and possible self.*

WRAPPING IT UP

As we have seen, non-events are part of everyone's story and, like most of life, come in a variety of sizes and disguises. That's why it may be helpful to ask yourself the following questions:

- *What are my dreams?* Since non-events are broken dreams or unmet expectations, this first question relates to what we expect. Generally, our expectations center on love, family, success, legacy, and self.
- *Where did my dreams come from?* Some of our dreams come from our society and various cultures, which have certain expectations and norms; others come from our own personal, individual lives; still others come from our family's expectations. The degree to which a lost dream is yours or someone else's dream *for* you will determine how easily you can give up the dream and reshape it.
- *How has my sense of* timing *been affected by my non-event?* Being off-time or late sets off a sense of failure and the realization that we are in the midst of a lost dream.
- *What triggers my awareness of this non-event?* There are many major ways we become aware of our non-events. The

triggers can be *external,* such as a colleague getting promoted; others are more *internal,* private, highly personal reminders that an expectation may never be realized.

❦ *What type of non-event am I experiencing?* Non-events can be *personal* ("I do not get promoted"), or they can *ripple* from someone we care about ("My partner does not get promoted and his or her depression affects me"), or they can *result* from an event that leads to a non-event ("We have no 'healthy' children because of giving birth to a multiply handicapped child"), or they can merely be *delayed.*

❦ *Are all my non-events "created equal"?* The answer is clearly no; they differ in many ways and their relative importance can be gauged by asking the question: Is my non-event hopeful or hopeless? Sudden or gradual? In or out of my control? Positive, negative, or neutral? Does it have a great or minor impact on my life?

❦ *How can I cope with my non-event?* It is not a specific non-event that matters, but the degree to which it changes your life, roles, relationships, routines, and assumptions. We also found that there is a way to reshape our expectations through a dream-reshaping process. (See Chapters 6 through 9.)

It is in that process that hope can emerge and in that striving that new dreams are found.

Identifying a Non-Event

PART II

in the

Vast Field

of Dreams

3

Love and Family

There are things we might tell

If there were someone to tell them to.

Instead, we tell them to ourselves,

Store them somewhere deep,

Keep our counsel.

These are the words unwritten,

The moments of life unshared,

That might have been letters home.

—SANDRA MEAGHER[1]

ot surprisingly, the unmet dreams of love and family can result in a sense of sadness, despair, and even betrayal when the expectations of intimacy are not fulfilled. That's because intimacy, in whatever form it takes, is essential to our well-being. Intimacy, however, is a two-way proposition, as Erik Erikson observed: "Intimacy . . . is the capacity for eventual commitment to lasting friendships and companionship. [It is] a mutual relationship of affection and trust that involves full appreciation of each other's uniqueness and separateness."[2]

In other words, we not only need to *have* loved ones and companions, we need to have the *capacity* to be close to others. Achieving intimacy is one of our earliest developmental tasks and the foundation of much that follows in our lives. Because intimacy can involve devotion to a partner, a close friend, a child, a parent, or a sibling, non-events in this arena may include a multitude of disappointments: never having had a long-term committed partner, living in a loveless relationship, or being unable to connect in a satisfying way to friends, parents, children, siblings, or other loved ones.

Sociologist Robert Weiss discusses two kinds of loneliness: social isolation (when we are cut off from community or a larger network) and emotional isolation (when we do not have one or two intimate others in our lives). Through studies of both couples and single parents, he found that just "as the provisions of marriage cannot be supplied by friendships, so too the provisions of friendships cannot be supplied by marriage."[3] Weiss discovered that people with partners but with a limited network of friends report as much loneliness as do people with large support networks but no intimate partner. In other words, people seem to need to be part of a social network, sharing with others the life concerns that are central to them, in order to experience social well-being. At the same time, adults also need intimacy with someone very close to them in order to experience emotional well-being at its deepest level. Weiss further found that relationships tend to be specialized in what they provide us and that, as a consequence, we need to maintain a number of different relationships for our well-being. The following describe the variety of these needs.

1. *Attachment* is provided in a relationship when each individual is mutually accessible to the other and creates a place that is constant and safe. These relationships usually occur in marriage, partnerships, or best friends.
2. *Social integration* is provided by those relationships in which the individuals have similar concerns. In this network of common concern, the members share information, ideas, and experiences. We'll see the advantages of these frequently work-related relationships when career non-events are discussed in Chapter 4.
3. *Opportunity for nurturance* occurs in those relationships in which we can care for our friends, family, and children. These are the relationships that make us feel that we matter because we are needed.
4. *Reassurance of worth* results when our competence is affirmed by the relationships in our family, community, or work.
5. *Sense of reliable alliance* is assured when we have continuity in our relationships with kin. These relationships, whether or not there are mutual feelings of love, provide us with a sense of being grounded.
6. *Obtaining guidance* refers to those relationships which afford us the opportunity for advice and counsel when we need it.

Obviously, in the best of life circumstances we will have a constellation of relationships that offer us most or all of these qualities. The constant for us as adults, however, is that we need both emotional and social connectedness. The way we achieve these may vary as our lives change and advance.

This framework is also useful for examining non-events and assessing which of our relational needs are not being met by the non-event. Many of these needs, as we will see, are particularly bound up with our lost dreams of love and family. For example, if an adult is struggling with the issue of infertility, clearly the need to nurture is at stake. On the other hand, if the network of friends diminishes sharply, then an individual's sense of worth, and even social integration, may be threatened. When you explore your *own* non-event, consider these same relational needs. In doing so, you'll find that the clues to your solutions lie within them.

WHEN ROMANTIC LOVE ELUDES US

In researching this book, we heard numerous stories about the search for love. Many (though by no means all) of these stories were from women who felt the span of their sexual appeal to be briefer than that afforded to men by our culture. As a consequence, beginning in their late twenties, several of the women we interviewed began to agonize over the absence of a permanent man in their lives.

Marlene reported: "I always thought I'd be married by age thirty, and it looks very likely that won't be the case. I'm twenty-nine and am not even dating anyone at the moment. What makes it difficult is that many of my good friends are getting married. Sometimes I feel like I'll never meet the right person." But, as we indicated earlier, many heartaches are linked to a social clock. If most of Marlene's friends were single and not dating, for example, she might perceive her situation very differently.

For some people, the absence of a mate may feel less a social failure than the result of "bad luck." As Brenda said: "I feel very successful in many areas of my life. I have a solid and happy family; I have always done well in school and competitive athletics. And I have always maintained the idealistic thought that I can have whatever I want as long as I am willing to work for it. However, I sometimes get stressed about finding the 'right' man, because it seems to be a matter of fate rather than a planned achievement or goal." When we can't seem to meet the right partner, despite our best efforts, even the most competent adult among us can begin to have self-doubts. At this point, our need for attachment spills into our need to be reassured that we are worthy.

To compound the problem, some members of certain racial and social groups seem to have a particularly difficult time finding a mate. On a recent television program, a group of African-American professional women discussed feeling "forced" to relinquish their dreams of romance. Like most women, they had expected to marry and raise families, but now deplored the lack of educated men with whom they could share their lives. The experts on the show noted that the ratio of men to women is especially low for this population, and the ratio of professional men to professional women even lower. Further, most interracial marriages are between white women and African-American men, not African-American women and white men.

Gwen, a thirty-five-year-old with a doctorate, described the pressure she felt to marry. Her parents constantly asked, "So what have you been doing lately?" which for this and many single adults has long been interpreted as meaning, "Have you met anyone 'important' yet?" Gwen confessed that she had begun to panic several years earlier when she didn't have a committed relationship. At the time, she hadn't related her situation to the larger demographic picture, so she blamed herself. Now, however, she is more at peace. She still wants to marry but has decided to focus in the meantime on her satisfying career, friends, and family.

IN SEARCH OF

Many respectable city magazines are replete with "ISOs"—the In Search Of ads in which many adults look for companionship. The following example is fairly typical:

> *An outstanding choice on your part deciding to answer this ad. I'm very bright, successful, well educated, athletic, and certainly attractive . . . I'm a 44-year-old DWM [divorced white male]— your age not as important as your mind, body, soul.*[4]

Sometimes these ads seem humorous or provocative, but frequently adults have few dating prospects at work or in other social settings. This lack should come as no surprise as single adults get older in a mobile, impersonal culture.

For Dora, forty-two, a high government official, the discussion of broken dreams was painfully close to home. When a three-year relationship ended, she was devastated and yet surprised at the depth of her reaction, since she had had many other relationships during her life. But this one ended when she turned forty. This particular birthday, coinciding with her failed romance, made Dora realize how central the desire for a permanent relationship really was for her. Despite an impressive career, she feels vulnerable to emotional isolation because so much of her energy has been spent on the fast track at work. Also as a result of this success, Dora senses that other women are jealous of her professionally, and men only regard her as a colleague, albeit an attractive one. Further, though she is perceived as successful by many others, Dora reports that she feels like a fraud because she doesn't have "what really matters." The reassurance of worth that this woman finds in the workplace is absent elsewhere in her life.

Dora's despondency has even led her to feel that her best friend, who is divorced, is better off because the friend at least has the status of someone who has been married. Dora wonders if she should abandon this dream of eventual love and a family.

Certainly there is no cut-off age for this kind of longing. As Monica, sixty-four, confided:

> *I always anticipated getting married. I grew up with the thought of a "perfect life" but came from a dysfunctional home. My last relationship ended when I was fifty. I reached rock bottom and was emotionally distraught. I began to wonder what's wrong with me? Maybe I never married because I was lacking in some quality, in the ability to stick to a relationship. On the other hand, I blamed my mother, who pushed me to only consider marrying a college graduate. [When I was younger] I went mostly with blue-collar men. This pressure to search for the perfect husband—both from mother and myself—influenced how I lived my life.*

Eventually, however, Monica took the situation in hand. "I realized that I was never happy, that I was always looking, always getting involved with the wrong men. Finally I went to a therapist and after four years of talking about this, I began to see that to be a whole person I did not need to be married." In her own way, Monica went through the dream-reshaping process described later in this book. "Once I realized that I could be single and happy, I totally revised my dream by taking direct action. After I went for counseling, I began to revisit the church. Today I am beginning to feel more spiritual, more whole. But I'm also having more fun, going out with friends and traveling a lot." Once she had let go of blaming her mother and feeling ashamed of her situation, Monica abandoned a dream that had left her miserable for years. At this point, Monica was able to provide for her need to attach, to interrelate with a broader group of people, and to feel valued and important in her community. As a consequence, she incorporated some of the best parts of intimacy by spending more time with her two closest friends, while expanding her network at church and in the neighborhood. In all, Monica reports that "emotionally I've never been happier."

Shanelle, thirty-eight, describes a similar transformation:

After my fiancé broke our engagement, I stopped being tentative and viewing my life as a prologue to meeting the right man. Unfortunately, around the same time, I also faced another blow—not getting an expected vice-presidency. The shock of not obtaining these two goals made me stop short and take stock. I began to revise my priorities and viewed my family and deep friendships as true gifts. Also I began to appreciate my independence and freedom and enjoy my status. That adjustment was a process that really began with the failed engagement.

Shanelle was also comforted to realize how many adults experience their own lost dreams. "It makes me feel less lonely to know that everyone suffers disappointments. It was that feeling of private shame that made them so hard to take."

Of course, women are not alone in seeking the perfect partner. Morris, busy caring for his two small sons after a divorce, definitely planned to remarry. His kids grew up and he kept looking. Despite all the articles about available women and too few men, Morris couldn't figure out where they were. He began to wonder if something were wrong with *him*. "I felt empty, incomplete, and discouraged when my efforts to have a relationship did not work out. Maybe it was the passage of time or the support of good friends, but I finally realized that life could be fun and that I could be complete even as a single man." Eventually, Morris began to relax and not approach every woman as a potential marriage partner. Today he is dating a woman for companionship and enjoying each day as it comes.

The Missing Mate

Most of us, whether by nature or culture, long for romantic love. From fairy tales in our earliest years to just about every song, movie, book, and ad that enters our consciousness, we dream of mating with the man or woman who will "complete" us. One woman, Pam, described her life in such storybook terms.

"My girlhood fantasies were filled with dreams about romance. Then, in college, I actually met the 'perfect mate.' He was handsome, on the road to success, and yes, in the end he was charming to everyone he met—except me." On the outside, Pam told us, their life was everything she had hoped for. The couple had money, status, and friends, but profound sadness was an undercurrent in her life. Her dream of being loved, appreciated, and "cherished beyond all others" was never realized, and her life became filled with a growing feeling of despair. Fortunately, Pam was a doer by nature. When she recognized the absence of love for what it was, she began to put her energy into community work. If attachment was not to be hers, at least she could work on social integration and find reassurance of her worth.

Still, adults can feel a low-grade despair when intimacy doesn't exist where it is expected. Perhaps this explains the tremendous appeal of the movie *Shirley Valentine*, which centers on a protagonist who finds it more satisfying to talk to the wall than to her husband. Here the husband and wife are inaccessible to each other, which leaves Shirley wondering: "When did I become 'she' instead of Shirley Valentine; when did my husband become 'he'?" For this character, attachment is missing, diminishing her feeling of worth. In the scenes that follow this realization, Shirley moves comically but surely toward reshaping her own dreams.

WONDERING WHAT MIGHT HAVE BEEN

At age twenty, Jeremy fell in love with Jenna, a girl he had met at a dance. When the relationship began to be serious, however, Jeremy set the terms of the relationship based on his firmly held religious beliefs. He insisted, for example, that any children born to them be brought up in his religion. When Jenna disagreed, he broke off the relationship. Thirty-five years later, he still thinks of her. For although Jeremy later married and had children, he never felt the way he did with his first love. Today he often wonders what life would have been like if he'd married

Jenna, and he blames himself for not seeking a compromise on the religious issue. In fact, non-events that once seemed in our control can sometimes be the most painful of all. These are the missed opportunities, the chances not taken when once the choices were ours. Dwelling too long on what might have been, however, can paralyze us. We need to learn from lost dreams like these and use them to shape our goals.

THE SEXLESS MARRIAGE

This phenomenon is apparently more common than most people realize, though a sexless marriage is only a non-event when one of the partners is unhappy with the situation. When this occurs, the unwilling spouse is left with feelings of shame, anger, and self-reproach as this secret non-event continues unresolved. In *Celibate Wives* by Joan Avna and Diana Waltz, one woman describes admitting her sorrow to a women's group only to learn that many in the group were also living in marriages without sex.[5] Most men and women, regardless of age, feel they have the right to sexual relations with their mates. The intensity and frequency of the relations may vary according to age, circumstance, or temperament, but that expectation is a given, albeit a seldom discussed one. When the assumption of sexual intimacy is unmet, the result is a non-event that demands some honest attention.

SUCH GOOD FRIENDS

In *Just Friends*, author Lillian Rubin suggests that friends are so important to us because they "provide a reference outside the family against which to measure and judge ourselves."[6] They are also often the ones who help us through a life transition, frequently sharing the same transitions themselves. Because a friend is freely chosen, not foisted on us by blood or mere circumstance, true friends provide a gift that few other relationships can offer. When we suffer a loss, sometimes an old friend can comfort us best, or sometimes we need the objectivity of a new friend who doesn't come laden with our painful memories.

Maggie cried as she described her son's death in January 1988. Had he lived and moved along on schedule, Michael would have graduated high school in May 1991. "I realize that friends with children my son's age are busy and excited with graduation plans. The death of a child is a lifetime of missed milestones—each one becoming a non-event of its own. His loss is always with me, but more so at birthdays, holidays, graduation times." Maggie suffers from recurrent depression and is very uncomfortable around people whose children had been Mike's age. Further, the opportunity for nurturance has been wrenched from her, and for a long time Maggie found little comfort in other relationships. In the ensuing months, Maggie withdrew from her group of friends whose children had gone to school with her son. Instead, she developed relationships at work and school—making friends with people who had no knowledge of her past. Though the loss still hurts, Maggie reports that this change in friendships was essential to her emotional stability as each resultant non-event presented itself.

More typical are adults such as Carlos, who swears by the friends who got him through the dissolution of his marriage.

> *When my dream of a loving marriage was shattered last year, my buddies were always there to help me out. They helped me move into a new apartment and dragged me out to ball games and things—just to get me out of my depression.*

Given the comfort it can provide, the breakup of a trusted friendship can be devastating. As with a marriage, we invest rather heavily in our closest friends, and when the friendship doesn't continue, the loss is usually more distressing for one of the friends. This shattered "dream of love" is all the more painful, in a way, because it is more private and inexplicable to others. How can we explain to anyone what a friend has meant? And how can we regroup from the hurt and let anyone be that close to us again when an earlier friendship is lost?

Friends have a place in the area of love, but friends might easily be considered in the context of family as well. The problem, as Rubin suggests, is that there are "no clearly defined norms for behavior or an agreed-upon set of reciprocal rights and obligations" for friends. Neither does our language distinguish between different types of friends—best friends, work friends, or social friends, for example. Best friends, in particular, hold a special place that is somewhere between love and family. As Rubin notes: "Best friends have the power to help and to hurt in ways that no one but a mate or a lover can match. Unlike other friendships, where expectations are more modest, we usually expect our best friends to meet us at many different levels."[7] For this reason, the absence or loss of a best friend may constitute a painful and trying non-event.

WHEN FAMILY DEALS US A NON-EVENT

Family. If ever a word evoked a mixture of feelings it's that one. Everyone has one or came from one, loved one, fought one, fled from one, defended one, renounced one, or cherished one. Whatever their flaws, we all dream at some level of the perfect family—ours. Unfortunately, if ever a group didn't meet our expectations and couldn't *hope* to meet them, truth be known, it's our families of origin and the families we create. Add to that the complexity of the modern family in flux, and family is a breeding ground for non-events.

FAMILY AND OTHER FORMS OF LIFE

Here's just a sample of today's family in flux: The once married may become the previously married; the heterosexual may emerge as homosexual; the never married may eventually marry, and so on. Furthermore, change can occur even if such designations as "married," "parent," or "friend" stay the same. Marriage, of course, goes through its own transformations; parenthood changes as both children and parents age; and good friends can become best friends, while best friends may revert to lesser status. And in the bargain, these support systems that meet our needs for attachment, alliance, and so on may be rocked at the foundation.

How does all this shifting and losing affect us? As sociologist Gunhild Hagestad remarks: "Shared understandings and expectations are often subtle and implicit. However, when expectations are *not* met and what was taken as given can no longer be counted on, the implicit becomes explicit, through strong reactions of 'this is not right!'"[8] We assume a lot from our families, and their non-compliance can provoke outrage and sorrow. That's because the understanding that we share with family members gives us a sense of the continuity and predictability that are essential to intimacy. For this reason, as we will see below, the betrayal of that understanding exacts a painful, if private, price.

The above only takes into consideration the "traditional" definitions of family. Just what *is* a family? Are lifelong lovers family? Are siblings with whom we don't speak family? Are best friends family—especially when they share our lives in ways our families of origin never could? Today, our understanding of family has expanded greatly, and with it, the possibility of lost family dreams.

THE FUTURE DEFERRED

If finishing school, getting married, buying a house, and having children are all part of the so-called American dream, then the signs are everywhere that this dream is increasingly delayed. Today men and women are marrying later; women are having their children later; more young adults take longer to finish their college degrees, while others continue to live in their parents' homes long past the typical time of departure; and many more adults are buying their first home at an older age. It seems that a combination of the tighter economy and fewer jobs has influenced many adults to defer careers, marriages, families, and major purchases.

Whatever the reason, adults in their twenties and thirties often label these delays non-events, expressing fear that the delays might be permanent. Ron told us:

> As a male in my early thirties, I think I have done some pretty exciting things in my life and have worked hard to get where I am. However, I guess I expected to be married by now. I have been putting a lot of energy into my career and have not put much energy into establishing a long-term relationship. My family sees me as a perpetual adolescent, saying that I don't want to be an adult and settle down. Sometimes I accept my role as a transient-adolescent. Other times, though, I wonder what is wrong with me. Holidays make me think about it more.

Lenore, thirty-seven, also worries about the delays in her life and is particularly afraid that she will never have a meaningful relationship. For the past year, she has been considering having a baby without a husband, fearful that the right man will never come along. Of course, these non-events may just be delayed events, and both Ron and Lenore need to be aware that changing demographics may be altering their lives—but not necessarily forever.

THE EMPTY CRADLE

Today roughly one in five couples will face infertility, with causes ranging from delayed childbearing, to not finding a suitable mate, to physical infertility, to "cause unknown." Whatever the reason, not being able to have children can be a traumatic non-event for many adults.

For many couples, part of the anguish of infertility is its continuing uncertainty. In many ways, the wait entails putting career and other life plans on hold and leaves the would-be parents in limbo: "Finding out every month that I am not pregnant when I expect and hope to be leaves me uncertain of the future," said one woman. "I don't know whether to ask for a promotion and now's the time to buy a new house. But will we need one?"

The anxiety of not conceiving a child led to the breakup of Tina's marriage. When asked how she coped with these two losses, Tina reported that she'd engaged in years of denial about their impact, followed by several more of therapy.

> It's hard to say when I first realized that the non-events of no children and a marriage that never "took" had left me devastated. During my denial phase, I kept really busy. I think it took years to begin to face my grief. Looking back, I realize I would have been helped if I had faced it all early on and labeled it.

Add to that the trend in marketing that seems to ignore women without children. *American Demographics* magazine reported:

> Children are so fashionable these days that non-parents are ignored. In August [1993], a slew of breathless reports focused on the rising proportion of unmarried women who are having babies. The articles were based on a new study by the Census Bureau, but they were not really news. The real changes have been happening among women who don't have children.[9]

It's interesting that such a national trend observer as *American Demographics* is mindful that childlessness (like other non-events) has more than one aspect, and not all of those aspects are negative:

There are three kinds of childless people—those who have no children yet, those who never will, and those whose kids have grown and gone. The day-to-day lives of the permanently childless may resemble those of pre- and post-parents, but their perspectives are very different. Non-parents never have to budget for diapers or college educations. They can make decisions about where to live without worrying about the quality of local schools or which pediatricians offer weekend hours. They can even experience parenthood vicariously through nieces, nephews, and friends' children—but only if they choose to.

Obviously, childlessness needn't connote infertility, nor is it simply a woman's issue. Reginald, who had always wanted to be a father, described his ordeal:

My wife had to take basal temperatures and record them on a chart, which made sexual intimacy seem more scientific and mechanical versus loving and natural. We began to focus on sex at the correct time of the month rather than on desire. My wife began to be depressed, and I reacted to that. The process of trying to have a baby was sometimes painful. My wife blamed herself and I began to doubt my manliness. The doctors have not concluded exactly why we can't get pregnant. How we will cope with it in the long run is uncertain. We could adopt but we have some fears about that; we could decide to have no children; we could try some other methods but we're afraid of those too. But my bottom-line fear is that infertility might someday lead to a divorce. I have never mentioned that possibility to my wife, but we seem to be getting on each other's nerves a lot and I worry if we can weather the storm.

Secondary infertility, or the inability to conceive a second child, produces a more subtle non-event. Leslie told us, "Although I had one child I expected to have more. In fact, I expected to be a mother/homemaker full-time, but I went back to work outside the home when I wasn't busy enough." For this woman, the move was a wise one. "As it turns out, I am really happy working outside the home. And it is probably good for my son, since he has a little more breathing room as I gained other interests."

MISCARRIAGE: THE SILENT LOSS

Miscarriage is often treated as if it were a non-event when, in fact, it is an event. Lorinne confided: "My miscarriage devastated me and I felt great grieving over the death of my child, yet it was not recognized as such. I was going to assume the role of new mother and suddenly that possibility was gone." Unlike Tina, however, Lorinne found her marriage strengthened by the loss. "Losing the baby changed my relationship with my husband. We grew closer as he shared my grief and I discovered how caring and supportive he really is. I only wish it hadn't taken a tragedy to bring us this close."

As Yvonne described her own miscarriage, she spoke of initial feelings of self-blame: "Though I know it was out of my control, I worried that I'd done something to cause it—I mean, by lifting something heavy, overexerting, being around chemicals for gardening." Then she recounted her changing reactions to the miscarriage. At first it was "horrible."

> I was depressed and cried all the time. I also carefully avoided friends who were pregnant. After several months, though, I began to see the miscarriage as a blessing in disguise. I got the courage to leave my marriage because my needs were not being met. If I'd carried the child to term I'd probably still be in a horrible marriage. I still want a marriage and child, though. I went into therapy and joined a support group. Now I'll see what develops.

Each of these women, however, felt the need to mourn her silent loss, to grieve for the baby that almost was, and to derive some good from the loss—if only to say that her miscarriage motivated her to leave a difficult marriage or to get into therapy or plan new dreams.

A DREAM TOO LATE

There are those who early in life choose not to have children but later regret it. When she was younger, Catherine had wanted to have a family, but she married late in life and her husband would not adopt. Because she was happy in her marriage, Catherine agreed and threw herself with new energy into her career. Since her husband's death, however, she both misses him terribly and mourns the lack of children in her life.

Lesley gave us another perspective on how complicated the question of delayed childbearing can be. Lesley had married for the first time when she was thirty-six, but wasn't sure she wanted children. "Two years later I had to have a hysterectomy. Now I worry I've let my husband down by not having children right away. The choice was once mine and now it is taken away." Even though Lesley had not planned on being a mother, she felt the loss keenly when the choice was no longer hers. She also reports a change in her social life. "We no longer socialize with people who have small children because it is too uncomfortable and I feel guilty that all our energy, time, and money is spent on ourselves. It has taken four years to recover from the realization that we will never be parents." Lesley described the process of adapting to her new situation in this way:

> When I saw the first friend who had a baby after my surgery, I cried a lot. With her second child, though, I felt better. I also saw a psychologist and talked with her about other regrets—about not having a child earlier with my college boyfriend, who died in an accident. My husband and I talk about our regrets, but ultimately we decided not to adopt a child. Very soon I realized that my sad-

ness resulted from many regrets about other lost loves and not get-
ting pregnant earlier. I was sad for about two years and coped by
eating too much. So now, older, wiser, and heavier I realize that I
need to take care of me and my health.

INFERTILITY AND SURPRISE ENDINGS

Another, happier story of the journey from infertility to
parenthood was recounted by Robin, a writer for a major daily
newspaper. A frank account of choices along the way puts the
loss in perspective:

> *That [five-year] quest took us through every diagnostic test and*
> *treatment then available. . . . Only toward the end of those years*
> *did I begin to grasp that what my husband and I were going*
> *through could stop, immediately, if we chose to stop. I could walk*
> *out of a doctor's office, get off of an examining table, cancel an*
> *operation at any point and say enough is enough. But how do*
> *you know when you've had enough of high-tech infertility treat-*
> *ment with its endless permutations? How do you find the courage*
> *and strength to say this is not working for us and we will have no*
> *more of it?*[10]

There were revelations along the way for Robin, including a conversation with another woman in a doctor's waiting
room who had been undergoing fertility treatment for ten years
and who had no intention of quitting. Robin was shocked by this
attitude and thought at the time: "No way am I going to be doing
this ten years from now. I will never let that happen to me."
Here's how Robin's particular story ends:

> *We had come to doctors for help in having a baby. The doctors*
> *responded with the only answer in which they are educated—*

medically aided conception. But there is a dislocation between what the doctor thinks his patients want—a pregnancy—and what the couple really has in mind—a baby.

There are other ways to create a family. Adoption, if it is mentioned at all, is offered at the end of (failed) treatment instead of as a positive option that can be pursued immediately.

My husband and I adopted our daughter, Eva, in December of 1987, and with her arrival the tenor of our lives changed dramatically—from a pattern of monthly grief, depression, and estrangement to pure joy.

A postscript to Robin's story was the surprise arrival of their son through pregnancy, but she adds:

We consider our son, Zachary, to be gravy on the delicious family life that Eva gave us. Only a small fraction of couples who adopt a child eventually go on to produce one themselves. The point is, we were already happy when Zachary came along. . . . And I can say, with the strongest conviction, that I love both of my children intensely.

THE INCOMPLETE FAMILY

At twenty-five, Brent spoke of his non-events with real sadness. Not having had a father or grandparents forms a major portion of this young man's discontent. It seems that Brent's father had gone to jail when Brent was too small to remember him and disappeared after he was released. All Brent's life he had heard about this exciting father who "went bad," and a part of him yearned to know and be with him. Another part of the family lore concerned his maternal grandparents. His grandmother, in particular, had been described to him by his mother, aunts, and older siblings as an extraordinary person, someone who held the immediate family together and cared for all the others. Interestingly, Brent talked more about the loss of his grandmother, partly because he had a stepfather but also because she represented what he imagined his friends and older siblings always had: unconditional love. As Brent put it, "Sometimes I wonder if I was born too late, but my family has always felt incomplete to me."

Marita's son, David, has a similar lament. Her first husband died when David was three and she eventually married a man older than her father. Marita is now forty-eight and separated from her second husband. David doesn't remember his father and sees little of his stepfather, who is seventy-three. When David asked in frustration one day: "Why can't we have a normal family?" Marita responded that there's no such thing. David, in turn, argued that all his friends have fathers and he hated feeling left out of "normal."

Even though Marita is correct that the typical family composed of a mother, father, and children living at home is far less typical today, most of us still hold on to that image. It's not easy to give up the myth of the perfect family—neither its shape nor its content.

Several adults spoke of a subtler absence: the parent who was present physically but not emotionally. Elizabeth described having a father "who could not connect with his children." Sadly, and perhaps unconsciously, Elizabeth married a man who doesn't connect with their children either. The impact of living with first a remote father, then a distant husband, began to wear on her. She has distanced herself from her husband and reports that she "no longer goes out of my way for my father. I only do the basics for him." Elizabeth described the dilemma of this kind of non-event well when she told us, "I assumed I would be loved and realized that cannot be, at least not in the ways I would wish it. The good part, though, is that this misfortune has made me much more open and loving with those whom I do choose to be close to."

BEMOANING THE SERPENT'S TOOTH

Parents in every age have held expectations about their children's choice of careers, mates, homes, even their personal grooming. But usually a parent's greatest, often unspoken, desire is to be loved by his or her children. In Shakespeare's *King Lear*, the daughters' greed and coldness grieves their aging father: "Sharper than a serpent's tooth it is to have a thankless child,"[11] mourns the king, a lament that every parent has understood at some time. In addition to emotional disappointments, sometimes parents have a hard time understanding their offspring's paths and decisions, choices that must clearly be the children's to make.

Milt confessed that it has been "the worst year of my life. Our son, who is twenty-five, told us he is gay. We are shattered and cannot and *will* not accept it." Of course, their son is crushed by his parents' response and keeps asking to talk about his life to his parents. Milt and his wife have chosen to avoid the subject, refusing to meet the son's partner and feeling "heartbroken that he will never marry and have children." Milt and his wife feel especially upset because their son is an only child. Typical of adults in denial, they feel they are living a double life, getting together with all their friends but not sharing what is really on their minds.

Less dramatic is the story of Sharon. She had given up her teaching career to raise children who, in her mind, would grow up to meet certain expectations. It's true that none of the children went to Ivy League colleges, nor pursued well-paying careers. But each has found a comfortable niche in life and is happily settled. Only Sharon retains a sense of discontent. As Sharon put it:

> I gave up my career to stay home and raise my children, but they did not turn out as expected. I had a picture of them with sweaters tied around their shoulders and going to eastern colleges. Instead,

one, who had to go to a special school, now works in a grocery store. Another dropped out of school and hasn't made a comeback. The third is a secretary. There is nothing wrong with them. I just spent my life expecting something different.

Many parents live vicariously through their children and suffer from non-events. As one father related, "When my wife and I go to parties it seems that everyone has children with fellowships to Harvard, Princeton, Yale, Barnard, and Bryn Mawr—that is, everybody but us!" It didn't occur to this couple that they were only hearing from those whose children were achieving (externally anyway) and living out parental dreams.

Further digging would likely reveal another side, as it did at a recent lunch at which three women met to catch up. One woman is an author, another a poet, the third is in retailing. Their children had been in elementary school together. At this annual gathering, the women discussed how unsettled they felt about their children's lives, especially about their "inappropriate" choices in lovers and partners—as these choices involved ethnic, class, and religious differences. The three mothers were also disturbed by their children's apparent lack of career focus. Further discussion also revealed concern about an abortion, suspected sexual abuse, and the seeming disarray in their offspring's lives. At every turn, it seemed, there were missed opportunities or delayed events, and these mothers were struggling with their own lost dreams as a consequence.

Another older mother, Etta, faces a different dilemma. At seventy-two, she longs for support from her family. However, her adult children are not there for holidays or her birthday, nor do they want her to visit and be with the grandchildren. This realization that the family is not close, that her children are not supportive now that she is older and in bad health, leaves Etta sad and depressed. What's worse, she blames herself. "If only I hadn't been so strict, sometimes even mean, maybe they would be here for me now."

WHEN PARENTS DON'T DELIVER

Sometimes adult children provide another perspective. Tucker, a man in his early thirties, protested:

> I was brought up in a traditional family whose culture stressed the importance of marriage and family. While I am highly successful professionally, the fact that I have not married and therefore have not had children is often stressful to me personally, primarily because it is a central concern for my family. The pressure from them to "do something" about my situation sometimes becomes a source of difficulty.

Barbara's situation was a little different:

> I'm thirty-eight, married for fifteen years, and have no children. Now I am separated. I have no regrets about my decision not to have children, but other people, especially my parents, have a lot of trouble with me not wanting a family. When I was younger, people were always telling me I would change my mind. Now that I'm older, people often feel it is not out of line to question me on my reasons. You'd think at my age that my parents would let me lead my own life without a running commentary.

THE SIBLING NON-BOND

As our parents age, siblings play an important role in our adult years, but increasingly in a mobile society that role is ill-defined. As a *New York Times* article recently concluded: "[Today] adult siblings inhabit a twilight zone of family relationships. They have no roles, no rituals, no clear-cut patterns of behavior, a few proscribed but no prescribed ways of relating—no relationship at all . . . since as freewheeling adults theirs is a voluntary association."[12]

Despite these ambiguities, however, the sibling relationship has the potential to be one of the most important during the adult years. Siblings share a family history, and thus can provide a sense of continuity and a reassurance of worth from our earliest years. For this reason, sibling non-events have the power to hurt us in ways that may feel uncomfortably familiar.

"It's not fair!" is one of the standard cries of childhood, and we heard several variations of that as we listened to grown siblings. Marci, for example, complained that her brother is never there when she needs him. She calls him regularly to describe their elderly father's deteriorating condition, but he never seems to have extra money to send, time to visit, or even the consideration to call. Marci says it would be easier to have no sibling than one who doesn't meet even minimal expectations. Art described his sorrow about his non-existent relationship with his sister. Art claims that she never participated in the care of their mother, yet took all the jewelry when their mother died, and now will not talk to him. Still another woman complained, "I do everything for Mother. Still she criticizes me for every little thing I fail to do but raves about John's monthly call."

Some sibling problems have less to do with rivalry than with a lack of closeness. Paolo longed to be close to his older brother despite their contentious childhood. He idolized his brother, even choosing the same college major, graduate school, and profession. Unfortunately, their respective career paths, a distance of five hundred miles, and the older brother's inertia all conspired to leave Paolo disappointed. "I had every reason to believe we would be close. I know it wasn't ill will on my brother's part. It's just left me with a low-grade hurt when I think of how good it could have been for us both."

GAY AND LESBIAN FAMILIES

In the realm of family, the absence of legal sanctions has created many non-events for gay and lesbian couples. Bette described her anguish at having no legal rights where her daughter was concerned. Eight years earlier, her partner had visited a sperm bank and conceived a baby girl. Together the couple had raised their daughter, living and sharing their lives like any other committed parents. However, when they separated, the biological mother refused to let Bette have access to the little girl. Because she has no legal recourse, Bette has been torn from the child who is her daughter in the most important way possible. But the law in Bette's case makes little room for love.

Ron, a young man in his late twenties, complained that he couldn't get coverage from his partner's health insurance. While the partner was an executive in a major corporation, Ron only worked part-time and couldn't get medical benefits on his own. Today that lack of coverage is still a major concern for this couple. Again, their non-event stems from narrowly interpreted laws.

In fact, the non-events of homosexual couples frequently revolve around the legal, political, and religious institutions that deny the reality of their lives. As with other families, gay families are also rich in their diversity. According to a study by psychologist Douglas Kimmel, 20 percent of gay men had been in heterosexual marriages and over half of those marriages produced children, while more than a third of the white lesbians and almost half of the black lesbians had formerly been married and had children.[13] Like heterosexual couples, gay and lesbian couples can be monogamous, unfaithful, happy, unhappy, devoted, contentious, and so on. The major difference, and the root of so many unmet expectations, is that heterosexual couples are protected by societal institutions and gay couples are not.

A FINAL CASE IN POINT

Most of the adults cited here sounded fairly clear about what dream was lost and how it made them feel, but this clarity usually only occurred after a fair amount of reflection and learning about non-events. This last story is more illustrative of adults who at first glance believe that love and family non-events bear no relevance to their lives.

Greta said she was so involved with her work that she had no time for non-events. She went on to describe a busy life of making speeches, attending conferences, writing papers, and giving classes, and it soon was clear that we wouldn't include her in our research.

Several months later, however, Greta called to say that she realized why she'd felt she had no non-events. She had only been thinking of her career during the discussion, and in that arena everything was happening as planned. But Thanksgiving had triggered the realization that she had a number of non-events, all in the area of family.

It seems that Greta had been part of a large family as a child, with a sister, grandparents, many aunts, uncles, and countless cousins. Secure in the love of her family, she went on to college and graduate school and then worked hard at her career. The years passed and Greta didn't marry until she was nearly forty, whereupon she had two children in rapid succession. As Greta was belatedly building a new family, however, she suffered many losses in her family of origin. Her sister died, her parents died, and one by one, her close aunts and uncles died. Despite these tragedies, her life remained complex and busy during her forties and fifties, as the children grew and her home and office bulged with activity. By Greta's mid-sixties, however, her children had grown and were living on their own, and she herself had divorced and moved to an apartment. Suddenly her life was quiet—much too quiet. At sixty-five, Greta became aware that she was part of a two-generation family instead of the four-generation one she had grown up in. True, most of her friends had lost their parents, or were taking care of ill ones, but these same friends had also acquired new roles as in-laws and grandparents. Because she had married and had children later in life, Greta found herself out of sync with her other friends and not meeting her own expectations of family life. As she remarked, "It seems that I'm losing, not acquiring new roles. I keep hoping that my children will marry and have children, and maybe some-day they will. Meanwhile, though, I feel like a walking non-event in this area of my life."

Greta's non-events were gradual in coming and certainly they felt out of her control. True, Greta didn't have a partner, but she did have three lifelong friends and a satisfying career. Not an exact substitute for a love relationship, they did provide a sense of reliable alliance, guidance, attachment, and competence. Missing, however, was an opportunity to nurture grandchildren. Fortunately, while Greta didn't have a larger family network now, this was still a possibility and one that gives her hope.

CONCLUSION

Even if the stories here don't fit you exactly, they exem-plify the wide range of love and family non-events.

As you reflect on your own story, consider these essen-tial points:

- ❦ It's not the specific family or love non-event that mat-ters, it's the impact it has on your life—on your relation-ships, routines, and even on the assumptions you had about yourself. A sexless marriage, or not having a baby—to name just two—will be perceived very differ-ently by different people. It is only the person experi-encing the non-event who can determine how critical this particular non-event is to his or her well-being. For some, these lacks do not change lives. For others, they lead to affairs, to divorces, to deception, to renewal. In a word, then, there's no correspondence between a partic-ular non-event and our reaction to it.
- ❦ Such theorists as Erikson and Weiss can help us put in

perspective why love and family non-events evoke such suffering. Erikson underscores the individual's struggle with resolving the capacity to give and take in mature, intimate ways. Weiss helps us understand that even if we have the capacity to love, to connect, we need multiple opportunities to be both part of a community and part of an intimate relationship. Taking a life-span approach, there will be many times when people feel their needs are being met and many other times when they are not.

❦ We can assess the degree to which our love or family non-event is hopeful or hopeless, in or out of our control, sudden or gradual. If there is hope, if we can control the non-event, or if we've had time to work things out, then we'll feel more positively.

❦ A possible course of action for dealing with non-events will become clearer in the dream-reshaping process described in the third section of this book. Meanwhile, when relationship non-events occur, we can examine them. Which "relational need" is being interrupted? Can we develop temporary networks and relationships? Can we diversify, so that even if we don't have a perfect situation, we can survive? Then maybe we can do more than survive—we can look to new vistas and find new ways to meet our needs.

Finally, as the stories in this chapter illustrate, many forces shape our dreams of love and family. And too often, as we have seen, these forces include what doesn't exist as well as what does. Indeed, there *are* things that we might tell if there were someone to tell them to, which is why we are grateful to those adults who shared their losses in powerful stories—stories that just might have been letters home.

4

The Dream of Success

This book [*Working*], being about work,

is . . . about a search . . . for daily meaning as

well as daily bread, for recognition as well

as cash, for astonishment rather than

torpor; in short, for a sort of life rather than

a Monday through Friday sort of dying."

—STUDS TERKEL[1]

areer. Work. Money. Recognition. For many adults, these words are loaded measures of their public success. Right or wrong, we are anguished when through downsizing or being fired, our careers are derailed; when after many years (or not so many) work becomes boring or dissatisfying; when our salary levels are lower than we expected; or when honors, awards, or promotions go to someone else. Is it any wonder then that success non-events can shake our self-confidence and leave us questioning our "worth"?

The news is rife with stories of government employees and elected officials whose careers are truncated by scandals—real or imagined. We read their stories with eyes of curiosity and sometimes we can even imagine their pain. But their public humiliation seems nothing compared to our own when work-related dreams are threatened. That became apparent as we listened to accounts of both friends and other adults in our research. Jack, for example, was a midlevel government worker who proudly received a Most Valued Employee award. Two months later, his job was eliminated. Harriet, a recent college graduate, is still sending out her résumé and circling the want ads. Seven months after graduation, she hasn't had a single "hot" lead. Judy has just been made manager of her division, but won't receive a raise for at least another year because her company is in financial trouble. Francis earned a master's degree in science and fully expected the celebratory party that all his colleagues had received. Weeks, then months, went by and no congratulations were ever offered. His dismay turned to embarrassment and ultimately to anger.

As adults, all of us need to be recognized and to feel we are competent and have purpose. For this reason, public or work-related non-events can deliver a great deal of discomfort and a sense of feeling exposed.

CAREER AND COMPETENCE

We usually associate heartache with love lost, not with a disappointing work life. But in fact we do experience a kind of heartache when our opportunities for purpose, competence, and a sense of mission and worth are thwarted. Psychologist Erik Erikson provides a framework for understanding why these work-related issues are so important. One of the early developmental stages, according to Erikson, revolves around "industry versus inferiority." This is the time when a child is generally in school, and such tasks as paying attention, perseverance, and handling many aspects of the culture are mastered. If these tasks are successfully completed, an individual develops a sense of purpose and competence—both essential ingredients for effective functioning in the workplace. The issue of work thus begins early, persists through our career lives, and remains an essential factor, even in retirement. That's why unresolved work-related issues can be traumatic. As Erikson wrote, "A separation from the work setting may engender a sense of inferiority by removing the individual from many areas in which he or she has participated with competence."[2]

Further, if the individual doesn't resolve these issues, there are "malignant" tendencies, to use Erikson's language. That is, in order to develop a sense of purpose, we must develop *initiative* within ourselves. If young people are complimented and rewarded for their initiative and industry, they flourish in later life. However, if individuals—probably as children—are made to feel guilty when they explore the world, as adults they will become "inhibited or ruthless," again to use Erikson's rhetoric, rather than productive and imaginative. The words "inhibited" and "ruthless" are somewhat sensational in their connotations. Yet as we interviewed many men and women, their own words reflected similar feelings of despair and anger as their dreams of success went unfulfilled.

SHIFTING TIMES IN THE WORKPLACE: TRANSFORMED ASSUMPTIONS

At one time, entry into the workforce, company loyalty, and a predictable retirement were the norm for most workers. No longer, as newspaper writer Peter Kilborn observed in an article on the changing workforce. "For all but the elite, work holds less promise, less purpose, less security and less dignity than it did a generation ago."[3] Kilborn further sets the context for career non-events when he notes that two of every five jobs in the United States are part-time without benefits. Today, our dreams of success are colliding with a disturbingly changed economy.

Still another article recently bore the ominous title "Graduates March Down Aisle into Job Nightmare"—a grim sign of an economic downturn in the marketplace. Ever wonder if your career non-event is completely your fault?

> *Take the case of the thousands who have had the misfortune to begin their working lives in a deteriorating economy that has cut a mean swath through the white-collar workforce. . . . Their voices . . . quaver with disappointment or resignation when they talk of what they are doing now versus what they expected, their prospects today versus those of friends just a few years ahead of them. . . . What distinguishes this recession from the last is the toll it is taking on white-collar jobs. In the 1981 recession . . . 838,000 new white-collar jobs were created while this time 209,000 have been lost.*[4]

Despite the statistics (and generally they aren't that helpful even when the statistic is you), the majority of adults need to work. And, until very recently, no one has challenged our belief that we also have the right to work. However, it's clear that today's career non-events are often shaped by forces outside ourselves. What were once reasonable expectations about work and success have clearly changed. Expecting to achieve a precise career dream, to do as well as or better than our parents, to move steadily up the mythical workplace ladder—all these goals may elude most people today.

Mary Catherine Bateson observes in *Composing a Life* that we have focused too much on the stubborn struggle toward a single goal rather than on the wonderful, if unpredictable, process.

> *We see achievement as purposeful and monolithic, like the sculpting of a massive tree trunk . . . rather than something crafted from odds and ends, like a patchwork quilt. . . . Graduation is supposed to be followed by the first real job, representing a step on an ascending ladder.*[5]

These assumptions, of course, are increasingly outdated, and the proverbial road to success is both jammed with traffic and under construction. Bateson captures the anguish of many adults when she reports that "many of society's casualties are men and women who assumed they had chosen a path in life and found that it disappeared in the underbrush." Theirs were not unreasonable assumptions; it's just that too many of our success dreams have been caught in the shifting times.

Marie, at thirty, reflects the keen frustration we feel when our old assumptions aren't met. A full-time college student who is working on a bachelor's degree, Marie reports that she's "still without a résumé or transferable skills" as year after year family demands have interrupted her goals. Like many of the men and women experiencing a career non-event, Marie needs to look closely at her dream and reshape the way she pursues it. At this juncture, however, she is filled with self-recrimination, asking us and herself, "Why is this process taking so long? Will I *ever* move into the system?"

MOVING IN: WHEN SUCCESS ELUDES US

Sometimes adults like Marie experience non-events because they are unable to move on to a new situation. Either they do not know *how* to get in, or their local economy is so shaky that good jobs are just unavailable. This can cause significant stress for the job seekers and surprising friction within their families. Charles reported that his unemployed stepdaughter is living at home and causing considerable irritation in the household. "Why doesn't Kathy get up every day to look for work?" he lamented. "She should be treating job hunting like a full-time job." Charles has clear expectations about how Kathy should handle this period in her life. But obviously she has other ideas (or maybe none at all) about how to cope with her disappointing status. Like many of us, Kathy grew up expecting a more direct connection between her formal education and a subsequent career. As a consequence, this career non-event has evoked in her a range of difficult emotions, including lethargy, depression, helplessness, and anger at her situation.

At this point, Kathy is discouraged and putting minimal effort into getting a job. But even an all-out assault on the job market may not yield immediate results. One woman confided that she had spent two years looking before she landed a job:

> I sent out 130 résumés; 102 were for professional positions and 28 were for secretarial positions. From the total of 28 secretarial applications, I received 9 job interviews. From the total of professional applications, I had 27 informational interviews, 9 job interviews, and the one job offer which I just accepted last week. In

the process of job seeking, I spent $973 on such things as trans-
portation, Xeroxing, stationery, and postage. I joined two job-
seekers' groups. During this period my total income was $10,148.
After my job-seeking expenses and monthly health insurance, I
had approximately $530 per month to live on. While I was
finally successful, the entire process was horrendous—both emo-
tionally and financially. It is very easy to understand why many
persons become discouraged and drop out. I have shared this story
to personalize the statistics and to clearly illustrate the difficulty of
the job-seeking process in today's labor market.

This story seems to carry two messages: First, in some areas of the country, the economy has created enormous obstacles to gainful employment. Second, with steady persistence and not a little ingenuity, the problem may eventually be solved.

Meanwhile, we need to cope with the inevitable stress of dreams that elude our grasp.

THE MISSING LAUREL

The shame many adults feel when they're unable to move into the job market is much like the humiliation that other adults report when they aren't chosen for public recognition, despite their obvious ability. One day you expect to get the award, the next day it goes to someone else. You're still the same person, but for a time you may feel differently about your life and about yourself. Like other competence issues, many of these experiences begin in our earlier years. Writing for *Working Mother*, one woman reported these painful episodes from adolescence:

Back in junior high school I was not chosen to be a member of the
National Honor Society. All of my friends were selected in a cere-
mony in front of the whole school. When the lights came back on,
they were all on stage and I was sitting in the middle of an empty
row all by myself. Although this happened so long ago, I still

remember my acute embarrassment. I could not talk about it to anyone and tried to pretend it did not bother me. But it really did.

I can [also] still recall. . . the disappointment I felt when I didn't make the chorus in seventh grade. I remember running to the school bulletin board, hoping to find my name among those who made the final cut. I reread the list, sure that my name would appear. When I finally realized it wasn't there, I scrawled a note to the music teacher. "There must have been a mistake," I wrote, "I'm sure I made the chorus. Please add my name to the list." For weeks afterward I rushed to check the bulletin board to see if my name had been added. It never was. I imagined the music teacher laughing at me for thinking I was a worthy candidate.[6]

There are probably few of us who have forgotten the success non-events of our youth—when not being elected, selected, or otherwise chosen for something we longed for left us publicly shamed in some fashion. Fortunately, this same woman used these and other experiences to draw a lesson for herself as a working mother: Just as the hurtful memories can stay inside us, so can the happy ones—a truth reinforced by her four-year-old son. One day the little boy unintentionally assuaged her guilt at leaving him at day care. Sure, he asserted, good things stayed inside of him because, "How else would I know you love me while you're at work?" Similarly, as we struggle with the supposed "disgrace" of lost success dreams, we may wish to hold on to our own good thoughts: about our lives, about our talents, about our *selves*.

As a high-school quarterback, Jason had thrown the losing pass in the last game of the season. That night, he came home very depressed and, as it turned out, with a concussion. Weeks later, at the football banquet, Jason was the only one of the star players who didn't receive an award—an omission that left him by turns feeling shocked, disappointed, shamed, and embarrassed. The next day he abruptly left school and went to his father's office, confiding that he couldn't possibly return to school and face the other students. Jason and his father went for a long walk, during which his father wisely told him that sometimes not getting our dreams can build character—even more than actually attaining our dreams. Although the truth of those words was lost on Jason at the time, he did return to school, and he eventually learned that the worst of the experience had been in his own mind. Still the public omission had stung, as these losses invariably do, and Jason remembers it many years later.

It is true that many of the non-events we've described are permanent. For example, for a high-school athlete, there's only one senior sports banquet. Once it's over, it's over. However, other seemingly lost honors may merely be delayed events. Marty's story illustrates this well.

> *I was turned down for a fellowship to graduate school when I was twenty-eight. I was depressed for months, but eventually had to bury the pain and settle for a dull job. I remember thinking that my future also would be dull and boring. At forty, I was able to pursue the degree I wanted. It's interesting. If you had interviewed me when I was twenty-nine, I would have been devastated by my non-event. Now, at forty-five, I see that what then felt like a forever non-event was just delayed.*

HANDS THAT NEVER ROCKED THE CRADLE

The absence of genuine nurturance during childhood, of course, can color a lifetime and account for some adults' struggles to move into a chosen career. As we noted in our discussion of Erikson, beliefs about our competence are established early on, and when these beliefs are tenuous at best, we may find ourselves hindered in realizing our best talents.

As a child, Jake had a major talent—his ability to sculpt. Though his family situation had been devastating, what kept him going was his dream of becoming a sculptor and creating a better world with art. With a mixture of pain and determination,

Jake summarized a childhood in which he had been abandoned twice. The first time was at age six when his mother died; the second was at age ten when his father left him with an aunt. As a teenager, Jake had to support himself completely and couldn't afford to pursue an education, much less one in art. He recounted his feelings surrounding this non-event:

> *I felt hurt by people not giving me a chance. I never married. I went through childhood and adulthood working. I never even gradu-ated from high school. I never felt loved, I never felt understood. This feeling of low self-esteem and needing to prove my worth is still with me. I am now seventy-one. I have had a hard life but I never gave up the dream of art. This year I sculpted one of the best pieces I've ever done and have sent pictures of it to many local gal-leries. Who knows where it will go, but I am in there plugging.*

Like the woman who spent two years in her job search, Jake is finally attaining his goal. But unlike this woman, his fail-ure to feel competent and purposeful as a child deterred him from his dream for many years.

MOVING THROUGH:
EVEN THE POPE PLATEAUS

Not only do people have clear expectations about mov-ing into career and success opportunities, they generally hope to advance once they're in a workplace. That is, people expect to move *into* the workforce and then *up*. According to Judith Bard-wick, who writes about the phenomenon of career "plateauing," people are stuck in the same job for several reasons: the structure of the organization precludes advancement; the content of the job is never-changing; or the content of the job is never-ending. First, we'll examine what Bardwick calls "structural" plateauing:

Of 100 people who are hired because they have all the right quali-
ties and look outstanding, only 10 will reach any level of middle
management and only 1 will reach the executive level. . . . [A]
typical organizational pyramid [has] a huge base, a fair middle,
and a little pimple on the top.[7]

In other words, an ascent through the workplace is the
exception rather than the rule because sheer numbers and the struc-
tures of most companies preclude all but a few from moving up.

TRAITORS IN THEIR MIDST

Occasionally, when people are "structurally" plateaued,
the loss may be caused by betrayal or backroom politics. For
Dottie, there was no question that this was the case:

I expected a promotion for which I was clearly the most qualified,
yet it was given to someone who lacked the required qualifications.
In fact, the position title I originally applied for was changed to
meet the selected applicant's current qualifications. This experience
made me lose respect for my superiors at work, but at times it made
me doubt myself. Maybe if I had been a more talented employee, I
would have been chosen.

Al's experience echoed these twin feelings of self-doubt
and resentment:

I expected to be promoted to the grade of colonel in 1975. The pro-
motion board met in August of that year and did not select me.
The prerelease chitchat that my name was not on the list of pro-
moters alerted me to what was to be the biggest surprise of my life. I
was not chosen. It was out of my control. I became very depressed
and I felt inadequate. When I found out that the board had been
compromised, I brought legal action against them, and fourteen

years later was retroactively promoted. But during those fourteen years I became bitter and disillusioned.

Tim also felt betrayed when he was "promoted" by his company to another department.

This change in jobs was portrayed as a promotion. But because of corporate red tape, I have not had a change in salary status. In fact, my alleged promotion has been treated as a lateral move. My trust in the company diminished as I feel a victim of a "bait and switch" tactic used to get me to join a new work team. My original enthusiasm for my job and this company have diminished considerably.

AN INHERITANCE LOST

Sometimes we can't move through a system that is closer to home. At fifty, Ralph was a somewhat reluctant adult learner who returned to graduate school to obtain a degree in engineering. Although returning students are becoming more the norm, Ralph found himself the oldest in most of his classes and having trouble with the workload. Most disturbing of all, his return to school had come as a result of a career non-event.

I had been "groomed" since childhood to someday run my family's company. I was cut short. All my adult life, the company and its demands and my position in the management of the company had been a given. My role determined my relationship to friends, suppliers, employees, friends, and most important to my wife and family. My father's precipitous selling of the business—a definite event—caused me to no longer have the role for which I had been groomed.

The resulting non-event forced Ralph to examine his life, his relationships, and especially his beliefs about himself.

You find out very rapidly who your real friends are. At home, it was confusing to my children. I suddenly went from being the provider to living in a period of uncertainty. Then, for want of anything better, I became a student. It was hard to suddenly have no office to go to every day. It also changed the way I saw myself. I had for years been the customer, not the vendor. I never had to sell myself before and I had no idea how difficult that is. Mostly, though, I had expected to peak in my business career by age fifty. Instead, I am embarking on a new career—engineering—and starting at the bottom as a student. In my case, failure of a long-expected event to materialize created more change in lifestyle, attitudes, social support than the occurrence of an event.

Fortunately, today Ralph has reshaped his dream. He has returned to school and works part-time as a computer consultant. He especially feels proud that he took the non-event, which presented a threat to both himself and his family, and reshaped his dream entirely. When moving up in one workplace proved impossible, Ralph moved out and into another.

REACHING FOR THE SNOOZE BUTTON

Not everyone expects to move up, but almost all adults hope to maintain some enthusiasm for their work. When this essential eagerness is eroded, we need to take a closer look at our jobs. Judith Bardwick, who discussed structural plateauing in an organizational sense, calls this problem "content" plateauing. That is, the content of our job becomes routine, even boring—a description reflected in an interview with Vince, a forty-three-year-old engineer:

I have a house, a mortgage, and I don't have the freedom to move. I come to work, I do my job, I get passed over for promotions, and I go home. Frankly, there's no challenge, no excitement at either work or home.

Vince is still struggling with how to recapture his old joy in life—on more than one front.

Mike, however, finds his own dissatisfaction is strictly work-related. As he explains, he has no expectation of moving up in the psychiatric hospital where he works. To begin with, at thirty-one, Mike lacks a college education and doesn't want to pursue one. Further, when managers and directors are hired at this hospital, they tend to stay in the organization, leaving little room for others to advance from lower-level jobs. Though Mike had realized this from the start, after three years he felt burned out as an orderly in the adolescent wing. Finally, he worked up his courage and spoke to his supervisor about a change to another part of the hospital. To his dismay, she became angry and told Mike he could leave if he didn't like his assignment.

It's clear, then, that career non-events can also stem from lost joy in the content of our work and from the feeling of being "structurally" trapped. Mike is debating how to change his situation without actually leaving the hospital or going back to school.

HINTS OF A WORKPLACE REVOLUTION

A few years back, *Fortune* magazine ran an interesting article that suggested a rising phenomenon: The typical white-collar worker was feeling overwhelmed, overcommitted, and undervalued, and was chafing at the feeling.

> *Stand by for a potentially major upheaval. Soon it could get a lot less fashionable to be overscheduled—to have too much to do, making sure of course that everybody knows it. The eighties saw heavy accretions in the cachet of long hours. ("My Filofax bulges more than your Filofax.") And now, with the recession, folks are troweling on the extra effort. ("If I've got this many projects under way, they can't fire me, right?")*[8]

Plateauing today thus has various aspects. It can imply being emotionally stuck in our perceived need to run faster in place to avoid being trampled. But this can lead to even greater stress, because overloading seldom pays off. What follows is a sense of being unhappy in our chosen careers, alienating our colleagues and subordinates, and giving the slimmest remains of ourselves to our families.

How does this emotional ceiling relate to career non-events? Frequently we hear laments like "I expected to be content, to enjoy work, but to still have time for the things I like to do. What happened?" Sometimes this less obvious non-event is of our own making, and that's when some adults began to examine their schedules and eliminate the real non-essentials: unproductive meetings, unnecessary projects and travel, and late nights at the office. As one supervisor wisely counseled a hard-driving employee: "You *can't* field every fly ball, so don't kill yourself trying." Often a strategy as simple as easing up on ourselves can rejuvenate our careers when job dissatisfaction delivers a non-event.

MOVING OUT: ON THE ROAD AGAIN

In most parts of our lives, there is a process of *exiting*, just as there's one of entering. Though we rarely articulate the last steps in our work lives until later in our careers, all employed adults expect to leave a job eventually—either for another job or for retirement from paid work.

In fact, as many times as we've moved into new jobs, new roles, relationships, apartments, cities, and so on, we obviously have exited from previous ones. When the expected exiting doesn't occur on schedule or in the way we expected, however, we may experience deep disappointment and feel that life is out of our control.

Let's take the example of retirement. Though the proportion of early retirements is increasing, there are still adults who want to retire but can't. This inability to depart from the workforce when the time feels right may not seem so disturbing at first. But imagine attending a satisfying movie, sitting patiently through the credits, and then preparing to leave as the screen darkens. For some reason, however, the exits are blocked and you are forced to wait indefinitely to vacate the theater. Gradually the satisfaction you had experienced from the movie starts to fade and a sense of being trapped begins to build.

Each of us has some internal calendar that alerts us when it's time to depart. This was true of opera star Beverly Sills, who told herself she'd stop singing professionally when she reached fifty. Since megastars book years into the future, Ms. Sills had planned carefully and honored her countless engagements before she graciously left that phase of her career. The same is often true for professional athletes and politicians, who have contracts and terms that obligate their commitment through a specified period—whether they feel like staying or not. Then they have the freedom to leave. For us lesser luminaries, a specific birthday (sixty-two or sixty-five, for example) is often the signal that a leavetaking is in order. Sometimes, though, financial difficulties preclude a scheduled retirement. Esther, sixty-three, continued to work at a tedious secretarial job, a situation necessitated by poor insurance and her husband's ill health. And Marla, a day worker with no health insurance but failing health, had to stay on the job until she qualified for Medicare. Each knew instinctively that she'd "stayed too long at the fair" and felt a keen need for exiting. By better planning, saving for retirement, and understanding the stress of "overstaying," however, these women began to alleviate the worst aspects of this particular career non-event.

SUCCESS AND INTIMACY: THE OVERLAPPING DREAMS

Although we separated our discussion of the dreams of success from the dreams of love and family in the previous chapter, they obviously overlap. Certainly one pervasive trend has expanded our possibilities for elusive success: Women have entered the workforce to stay—a phenomenon that has proved a boon for most women, while leaving them open to the same job vulnerability as men. On the plus side, researchers in one study found that women's well-being was tied to fulfilling both intimacy *and* competency needs, and that the latter was true whether the women were married, divorced, or with or without children.[9] The researchers further observed that those women in the study who had multiple roles, that is, who were homemakers and workers and mothers, were more satisfied. But they were often, the researchers found, more challenged.

This was dramatically seen in a recent workshop for women professionals in which work transitions were explored. It also became clear during this day-long session that it was impossible to discuss work without noting how family can conflict with our careers, as well as enhance them. To cite just two examples: One woman, a midlevel manager, described her former ideal life—a husband, a little girl, two pets, another baby on the way, and a career in which she was advancing. Everything changed, however, when their second child was born with severe disabilities. At this point, the woman reduced her work to part-time and became absorbed in orchestrating family tasks and schedules that revolved around the baby. A second woman, just offered the job of office manager, suddenly became a single parent. Her best friend died, and she became the guardian of an eleven-year-old boy. At that point, she declined the promotion, feeling too overwhelmed with her new role as a parent to undertake another set of work responsibilities. Life circumstances forced each woman to rearrange her work life, which in turn resulted in a career non-event.

At another workshop, with postal employees (all of whom were managers who had started at the bottom), we saw that family and career issues likewise overlapped. Gary, forty-six, spoke of the opportunity he had been given to move to Norman, Oklahoma, the training headquarters for the postal service. His wife bitterly resented the move, and while she did eventually move with him, they were divorced within two years. As family and career dreams collided, Gary's expectation of permanency was interrupted. Leonard, another member of the workshop, described disasters in his own marriage as precipitated by his drinking. Eventually, Leonard joined Alcoholics Anonymous and received considerable support from his work team and manager. That support enabled Leonard to cope with both alcoholism and conflicts in his home life while continuing to be productive. In Leonard's case, career and family dreams stayed relatively on course with additional help.

For most men and women, in an endless combination of circumstances, the issues of nurturing and intimacy, careers and advancement will often intersect.

HIS WORLD, HER WORLD

It's not uncommon for spouses, usually women, to prepare for a career and then find it impossible to work at their professions because their partners' professional needs come first. Some women say they freely choose to subordinate their careers, while others only do so out of obligation.

In the past, women's primary dream was of family and men's of their careers. Even when more women began to work outside the home and men took new interest in parenting, the preoccupations of each sex remained in separate areas. Now this is changing for several reasons.

First, more women work for pay, even women with small

children, and it is generally assumed that these women will work during a longer portion of their lives. Consequently, women are heavily invested today in both family *and* work. Second, men's roles are also changing. Today more men find satisfaction in their personal relations. Women still carry the greater workload when it comes to family and household tasks, but various studies indicate that increasingly both women *and* men find significant psychological and physical well-being in connecting closely with their families.

Third, men and women in later life exhibit increasing possibilities for expansion and development, with men becoming more caring and women more achievement-oriented. Still, the usual stereotypes of aging, depletion, and loss persist, according to psychologist David Gutmann, who debunks these myths with "striking evidence of new development in both the male and female personalities in later life, the emergence of new executive capacities that go beyond mere adjustment to imposed loss." Through cross-cultural studies of younger and older men and women in a variety of societies, Gutmann further confirmed his hypothesis that older men acquire "softer" qualities of affect and cognition, while older women appear to move in an opposite direction, as they "embrace the aggressive masculinity that the older men are relinquishing."[10]

Edwin confirmed the truth of this tendency for men to develop in new directions:

> When I was forty-five, the most important thing in my life was arguing a case before the Supreme Court. Now, at sixty-five, scheduled soon for open-heart surgery, the most important thing in my life is my family—my wife, my children and grandchildren. It's not just fear of facing my mortality. Somewhere along the line, my values seemed to change.

Thus, family and love non-events will take on an increasing salience for men just as non-events in career areas will become increasingly important for women. Our cultural dreams are shifting, it seems, and our sex-role dreams along with them.

SEX-ROLE BIAS DIES HARD

In discussing the shifting roles of men and women, we still need to acknowledge the very real persistence of sex-role bias in the workforce. Though we think of such bias as a political or workplace issue, like most biases in life, the preferential treatment of one sex over the other frequently begins at home and quickly moves beyond the allocation of chores. Such partiality, unfortunately, can have lifelong consequences related to moving into an educational or workplace environment.

Angela and her brother had both wanted to become doctors since they were small, a desire that was still with them when each began making plans for college. Unfortunately for Angela, now middle-aged, her father felt that only his son should become a doctor, and Angela was forced to enter nursing, a profession, he told her, that was "more suitable for a girl." Naturally it came as a double blow, years later, when her brother chose to drop out of medical school.

Dorothy had always dreamed of singing professionally. As a child, she spent Saturdays at the opera and listened to opera music constantly. But her dream of studying music was never achieved because her family's financial difficulties precluded "educating a girl." Later, after she married, Dorothy was able to afford a year of voice training and auditioned for a choral group. Though she passed the audition, Dorothy eventually dropped out because her sightreading was inadequate. Now in her late seventies, she feels frustrated that her considerable talent was never developed.

We rarely heard from men whose dreams were challenged because of their sex, although we know a male nurse and a dancer who have their own stories of disappointment to tell. Still, men and women are expanding their options in the public world of success—and sex-role bias in the future, we suspect, will keep very few of them down.

MOVING IN, OUT, THEN UP: ONE WOMAN'S STORY

Sometimes a constellation of factors conspire to keep us from attaining our careers. For Julie, those factors included family, sex, culture, and a run of bad luck.

> My husband and I have both traveled widely, so his career with a branch of the foreign service seemed ideal for us. But from the beginning, our assignment in the Dominican Republic was a disaster. As a spouse, I was given no language training, no employment, no status of any kind other than that of a dependent. Here I was, a trained teacher, a former exchange student with a lot of overseas experience, and my only options were to play bridge at the Women's Club and "behave" like the other wives.

> What triggered my realization that I was in the midst of a devastating non-event? This will sound ridiculous, but the trigger was a piece of candy. One day, my husband came home from work and mentioned that someone had left a piece of candy on his desk. The candy meant nothing to him, but to me it said that he'd been accepted, that he was part of this post now, that people liked him, and that he fit in. I still remember the impact that gesture had on me, and I knew from then on that I couldn't continue in that situation. I went from viewing myself as a capable teacher to feeling like a non-person . . . like an appendage to another human being.

For Julie, the candy triggered the realization that her situation was untenable *and* that her life would have to change. At first, she felt helpless in a system over which she had no control. But eventually Julie's inability to obtain work, to feel useful and

GOING TO PLAN B

productive, led her to leave the system and regain her life. Julie described her coping process.

> Fortunately, I'm very goal-oriented, and when it was clear that none of my attempts were helping, I began to try other strategies. First, my husband and I discussed my returning to Oregon, where I would take classes and broaden my skill base. It was hard to leave him—if even for a few months—but we agreed that I couldn't continue in that situation. Our phone bills were horrendous—six hundred to seven hundred dollars a month for eight months—but we are each other's best friend and we needed to be in touch daily. While in Oregon, I contacted the Peace Corps to see if I could be a volunteer in the Dominican Republic. That way, my husband and I could be together at his assignment and we could each be productive in our different careers. The Peace Corps finally accepted me. But when the assignment came, I was stationed two whole hours away from my husband. Finally, having tried every avenue we knew to be together and have careers in the Dominican Republic, my husband requested a return to Washington, D.C.

Fortunately too for Julie, the experience wasn't wasted. In fact, she found that it strengthened her marriage, her self-confidence, and her belief in improving almost any situation.

> This career situation was extremely difficult for over two years, but I learned a lot from it. I also learned that I'm an individual who needs to conform to no one's standards but my own. The experience cemented my relationship with my husband, but mostly it made me feel wonderful about myself and my ability to grow and revise my dreams.

Julie's advice for others in similar circumstances:

> My message to others is straightforward. First, talk to others. We need to find kindred spirits when we're experiencing a lost career

dream, to avoid isolation when things seem the most bleak. We also need to take control of our situation. I also found it helpful to make a list of what's wrong when I'm upset. Then I can come up with strategies for changing the situation. I also placed time limits on external circumstances. For example, I told the Peace Corps I needed a final decision by such-and-such date. That way, I didn't drag out my frustration forever.

THE MEANINGS OF OUR SUCCESS

As we reflect on coping with career non-events, Mary Catherine Bateson's work is once again instructive. Bateson suggests that "it is time now to explore the creative potential of interrupted and conflicted lives, where energies are not narrowly focused or permanently pointed toward a single ambition. These are not lives without commitment, but rather lives in which commitments are continually refocused and redefined."[11] In fact, perhaps the most important way to cope with career disappointments is to rethink our definitions of success, to question their source, and to start living our own scripts rather than the supposed scripts of others. Kurt chose to do just that.

RIGHT GUY, WRONG PATH

Kurt disclosed that his onetime dreams of success seemed to have come from television, his parents, and society in general. As he summarized his thoughts of the past several years, Kurt offered this advice.

First, reexamine your beliefs about what you should do in your career versus what you want to do. Then think rationally about other career possibilities that would be more suited to your temperament. Above all, you live best by listening to your own expectations.

Kurt's story is also not atypical of the eighties. At thirty-five, he agreed that his expectations had indeed been shaped by the kinds of career moves that the movie *Wall Street* described. Like many young men with ambition, Kurt had expected to move quickly into a six-figure salary and, during the stock market heyday of the eighties, he did. Then came the "crash" in October 1987 and the corporate world became a different place. Many young stockbrokers were laid off, even bought off, as one by one the major financial firms realized they had overhired, overpromised, and overpaid a generation of expectant young men and women.

Kurt's chosen field had been real estate, where similar expectations of wealth had permeated his own dreams of success. Kurt describes his situation like this:

> *I hoped that I would come out of college, go into the field I had studied for, and stay. But more than that, I expected that I would find my niche and be on the fast track. Making a lot of money, like my stockbroker friends, was important, as was succeeding in the field I had chosen. But the longer I stayed in real estate, the more I realized that I hated it. I was even pretty good at it, but I really, truly hated it. And yet I felt that I was supposed to succeed at this career. Make a lot of money. Be terrific in sales. Added to that was the fact that my wife and her family are in real estate too. My wife loves it and she's been very successful.*

But being in the wrong career for all the wrong reasons began to affect Kurt seriously in his personal relationships. He continued:

> *I began to realize I had a problem when I began to get angry at people—usually my wife. But I also found I was difficult with other people too, and I developed a real self-esteem problem. Finally, I took a course on adult development and I began to think about what I wanted. I wasn't ready for a move yet, but this got*

me thinking. I guess you could say the realization that I was experiencing a career non-event was gradual, but the trigger was writing a paper on the dream in adult men's lives. Like other guys my age and in my circumstances, I expected the fast track and money to happen right away. I saw other guys achieving what I had expected of myself and this made matters worse.

Then came the turning point for Kurt:

One day, after a particularly difficult argument with my wife, I just walked into the office and quit. Just like that. I thought it would be hard, but all I felt was relief. While I am still formulating how I feel about myself after this major upheaval, there's a part of me that still believes I should be like everyone else and "succeed." On the other hand, I feel a lot of freedom from the knowledge that I don't have to be like others. That I can succeed at things that I want. And that success isn't measured by money or fierce competition. This experience made me know I had to follow my own dreams—not my wife's, not my in-laws'—but mine. I hope I can continue to slow down, reassess, and follow the dreams that emerge from within me.

Like Kurt, we will sometimes be faced with stressful choices. But whether we freely or grudgingly give up a career for another person, or leave a situation or economy that precludes our pursuing a dream, we each have one lifetime apiece. Bemoaning that fact is useless, and moving on doesn't imply giving up. Rather, it may mean we must relinquish some old assumptions—including one of education leading to one career that fulfills an entire adulthood. With that realization, we begin to invent and *reinvent* ourselves, knowing that our larger search for meaning both links and transcends our public lives.

5

Self and Legacy

To find in ourselves what makes life worth living is risky business, for it means that once we know we must seek it. It also means that without it life will be valueless.

—MARSHA SINETAR[1]

Perhaps immortality, too, is part of the quest. To be remembered was the wish spoken and unspoken, of the heroes and heroines of this book.

—STUDS TERKEL[2]

For most of our lives, we seem to harbor conflicting longings. To begin with, our dreams of who and how we should be are often at variance with the reality of our best selves. Then, as we come to the end of our lives, our dreams of having truly mattered and leaving behind a rich legacy are bound to another host of "shoulds." It seems that too often in this business of having and letting go we come out the losers, never quite measuring up to our own impossible standards. This is true as we consider our present and future selves, the latter being the imagined memories that we anxiously hope will survive us.

So what are the paths (for clearly there are many) out of this dismal forest? How can we embrace and realize our present selves? And how shall we maintain this fragile yet vital hope that our lives do and will matter today and into the future—even a future that ultimately will be without us?

THE ME NOBODY KNOWS

During the early seventies, a musical appeared on Broadway entitled *The Me Nobody Knows.* The score was created from a collection of poems written by disadvantaged children, and the musical was enacted by children of white, Afro-American, and Hispanic origin who closed with the song "Let Me Come In." This is an anthem that we well might sing to ourselves, for, as we will see, we are often our own greatest obstacles to realizing the very personal dream of self.

Self-censure and reproach can take many forms, as was evident in a Labor Day gathering of adults who played a game they called "What I *Didn't* Do This Summer." Though the intent was clearly playful, the individuals were quick to respond with what sounded harshly like self-criticism, citing such examples as not finding a companion, not sticking to an exercise routine, not taking a vacation, and even not learning to play bridge. Though exercises like this can be an amusing way to both reflect on the past and imagine a generally more disciplined future, the most telling parts of such conversations pertain more to doing than to being. Yet as one counselor we know gently advised a client: "We don't ask that beautiful paintings do anything. The fact that they *are* is sufficient. So too with each of us."

But being and doing are rarely separated in our psyches—a misfortune of our Western culture, where "What do you do?" not "Who are you?" is always the leading question. We like to think that the former is more appropriate and courteous, but the fact is that too few of us ever answer the latter question to anyone—least of all ourselves. Thus *what* I do is allowed to define who I *am*, rendering self non-events some of the most pervasive, if subtle, ones in our lives.

However we divide the idea of self, this sense of individuality is so intimate to our being that often we're unaware that we have enormous self-expectations. But this concept of self— both the momentary experiencing of our individuality *and* the more objective attributes by which we describe ourselves—is key to how we weather any adversity. As many adults related their life disappointments to us, many acknowledged that they'd lost the *idea* of self that had been part of their identity. Much of that identity was about *doing*—becoming a parent, entering and rising through the workforce, or acquiring material possessions that would make life easier and more pleasant.

But others warmed to discussing a deeper sense of loss, including their perception that what they *were* was not sufficient. The failings were expressed in a number of ways:

- ❦ I am not a generous person. When my mother was ill, my sister did most of the caretaking.
- ❦ I don't feel as vibrant as I used to. Some of my spark is gone.
- ❦ I'm disappointed in myself for having petty thoughts about other people, for envying and criticizing them.
- ❦ My siblings are smarter than I am. Even though I'm successful, I feel like the intellectual dud of our family.
- ❦ I wish I were more loving. Mostly I'm shy and worry about how I'll come across to others. I rarely think of their needs first.

The list of our self-doubts and misgivings can wear us down with its variety. That's because the person we imagined ourselves to be is in many ways more crucial to our well-being than our external achievements. Often it's easier to concede that we couldn't conceive a child or get a particular job than to admit that we are disappointed in our very selves.

Lest we think, however, that dreams of self are all negative and that we seldom become what we desire, we must remember the countless adults who have grown wiser, stronger, gentler, and sometimes more successful than ever they imagined. The ending of Betty Friedan's book *The Fountain of Age,* for example, reveals a sense of self that is at once realistic and joyous:

> *I realized that all the experiences I have had . . . mistakes, triumphs, battles lost and won, and moments of despair and exaltation, are part of me now:* I am myself at this age. *It took me all these years to put the missing pieces together, to confront my own age in terms of integrity and generativity, moving into the unknown future with a comfort now, instead of being stuck in the past. I have never felt so free.* [3]

It is the inability to achieve this freedom that makes many of us so profoundly disappointed in ourselves. Clearly we don't need Friedan's fame to experience such exhilarating peace. But we do need to integrate the various "missing pieces" and then embrace the whole, however odd in shape.

Because we are so varied in our humanity, there are countless images of ourselves we might hope to project. Generally, though, these dreams of self focus on physical, intellectual, emotional, and spiritual issues.

OUR IMPERFECT BODIES

Is there a woman alive who at some time has not agonized over being the wrong weight or shape, or over not being attractive enough? And what of the men who have wrestled with self-image related to complexion, height, baldness, or general lack of physical prowess? Less numerous, or at least less obvious, are those of us who wrestle with imperfect health—the diseases, conditions, and predispositions that play subtle havoc with our self-esteem and sometimes major havoc with our very lives.

This constant comparison, perpetuated by ads reflecting an arbitrary standard of beauty, keeps many "body non-events" alive for the vast majority of women. Just the other day we heard that a friend of ours had complained to a friend: "I am a diet junkie. I've been to Weight Watchers, Diet Center, Nutri System, and none of them work. My nails have grown, my hair is great but why can't I get thin?" Her friend reportedly answered: "Maybe it's time to change your image of the perfect you. You're in good health and you look good, so why aggravate yourself?" Refusing to let go of her self-torment, however, our friend responded, "I can't help it. It is the one area that seems out of my control. I think about it every day. I know the reasonable thing is to either diet and lose weight or change my image of myself. The way it is now, I am never satisfied. If only I could do as you suggest and forget the whole issue."

After years of similar self-torture, Celeste found comfort in visiting a museum of fine arts. Noting the variety of beauty through the ages, whether depicted by El Greco or Giacometti, with their long, angular subjects or by Rubens, Monet, or Rodin, whose figures are fleshy and round, Celeste began to regard her own body with a kinder gaze. Knowing too that her face wasn't "classically" beautiful, she found Modigliani and Picasso in one of the galleries and was pleased by the artists' rendering of faces of even less conventional beauty than her own. In fact, Celeste recounted, none of the greater artists diminished the individuality of their subjects by "airbrushing" away their so-called flaws. Rather, each subject was depicted as the artists beheld them—with reverence and delight.

MIND OVER MATTER

Some adults very privately lamented their lack of intellectual ability—or their *perceived* lack. For a few, this became a powerful intellectual non-event. They had dreamed of at least keeping pace with classmates and colleagues, and they secretly feared they never would. Todd, now forty-four, vividly remembers his brother and sister bringing home straight A's and the shame he felt at his own lackluster grades. As the third child in his family, he not only had to contend with the delayed ability that sometimes befalls the youngest but also found school an arena for failure. Though immensely successful in a real-estate career today, he still recalls feeling inferior to his siblings and many of his classmates.

We're just beginning to understand, however, that schools too often have failed youngsters like Todd, not the other way around. Further, educators are learning that there are many kinds of intelligence besides that equated with academic skills, including musical intelligence, spatial and artistic intelligence, common sense, and social intelligence. In addition, we know that some people are primarily visual learners, others aural, and still others kinesthetic, that is, they learn by *doing*. We also have learned that a host of learning disabilities can interfere with a child's academic learning. These range from dyslexia (difficulty with reading), to dyscalcula (a genuine difficulty with math), to dysgraphia (difficulty with writing that goes beyond bad penmanship), to various versions of Attention Deficit Disorder (ADD). But many adults today are products of schooling that labeled, tracked, punished, and showed little understanding of the variety of children's needs and learning styles. For too many, this scholastic deficit has been internalized as theirs alone—a misperception that can cause undue anguish even years after leaving school.

Not all our "intellectual non-events" originate in childhood, however. As they age, many adults fear that their learning capacity will diminish, an expectancy that even prompts some to change their life plans. Take the woman who claimed, "I'll be sixty-five in two years and by then I will have lost it!"—as if some biological calendar required a dip in IQ. And we've heard other older adults repeat a variation of this lament many times. "My memory is beginning to go." "I can barely remember my own name, much less consider taking a class."

Fortunately, new research on cognitive capacity challenges the assumption that our minds invariably fail as we age. Quite the contrary. In recent studies, gerontologists developed programs that train older people to solve problems more effectively than they did when they were younger. This research also points to a new way to view aging: As we grow older, if we receive the proper stimulation and training, "intellectual *plasticity*" is possible—that is, declining mental functioning can actually be reversed.[4]

These studies send a clear message: As better health care, extended life expectancy, and better living and learning conditions are made available to adults, those expecting to decline are surprised to discover more, not fewer, possibilities. For even older adults can grow in problem-solving ability and wisdom, if not in their speed or absorption and retention of irrelevant facts.

Sometimes, then, we expect an intellectual *event*—mental decline—and to our relief and delight it doesn't happen. For this reason we must change some deeply held convictions about our own aging. Of course, many of us begin to be more forgetful and to slow down a little, but in general there are new gains in problem-solving ability and wisdom to compensate. To conclude, then, today we can no longer look at fifty-, sixty-, or seventy-year-olds and make assumptions about their intellectual capacity. Nor can we assume that all non-events are losses. In areas that affect our sense of self, some of our lost dreams are clearly based on false information or cultural bias, which in turn creates the artificial standards, measured against which we invariably lose. Think that you're wanting intellectually? Think again.

THAT ELUSIVE INNER PEACE

A common belief is that we mellow as we get older, acquiring knowledge, insight, prudence, and wisdom as we advance in age. So why, we might wonder, isn't that happening to us? Many of us hold to a notion of adulthood as a time when everything settles, when the agonies of adolescence are over. And the tasks of adulthood, we reason, should result in inner peace. Naturally when that doesn't occur, we blame ourselves.

Harold, now a CEO, had always expected to be a leader —he is. He had always expected to be a father—he's that too. He had always expected to be a husband—he has been, two times. So what is missing? Why is he feeling consumed with negative feelings? For the past six years, Harold has not been speaking to his parents, angry over verbal abuse from both his mother and father that began in his childhood. Unable to let go of this fifty-year-old anger, however, Harold also finds himself angry at his siblings, who continue to see their parents. But secretly, he feels ashamed that he hasn't "developed" emotionally as well as he has in other aspects of his life. Faced with this internal dilemma, Harold is experiencing a sense of despair rather than the sense of integrity that Erikson asserts should mark our later years.

Marilyn too seems to have it all. At seventy-two, she is still attractive, she has a wide network of friends, and she teaches and consults in a field that intrigues her. Yet Marilyn feels she is living a lie. The discrepancy between how she is seen and how she feels about herself makes her feel unsettled and foolish. Beginning in the seventh grade and continuing even today, Marilyn has judged herself against one friend in particular who has more—more money, more status, more friends, better jobs through the years, and now more successful children. In fact, Marilyn always seems to choose friends who ostensibly have "more." When she was thirty, Marilyn reported, she expected to grow out of these feelings of envy and jealous competition. Somehow she never did. Now, to add to this emotional regret, Marilyn doesn't share these "shameful" thoughts with anyone, and feels both inferior and ashamed of feeling inferior. Surely, she had thought, as I get older this needy side of me will slowly wither. But Marilyn is still consumed with feelings of jealousy and concern for others' opinions. How can she begin to accept herself? What does she do with the emotional non-event of not becoming comfortable with herself? As another man lamented: "When will I get over my childhood traumas? I can't seem to let go of my anger at my father. But until I do, I can never be free."

In the emotional journey of our lives, ultimately all roads should tend to this inner freedom. When we realize the best dreams for ourselves, we will understand the Buddhist tenet (echoed in some way in every major religion) that all suffering comes from desire. In a more Western sense, we may understand this as desire for revenge, beauty, achievement, power, fame, and so on. But divesting ourselves of old sufferings can be a life's work. In the dream-reshaping process, we'll consider several approaches for assisting our emotional selves, approaches that may ease this divestiture and help us, in the best sense, to be free.

OUR SPIRITS, OUR SELVES

The spiritual world is one that we sometimes sidestep in this country, the way one avoids unpleasant sections of town or neighbors who are, one hesitates to say, slightly odd. In fact, except for publications that clearly are New Age or religious, we tend to find it bad form to bring up God in polite company— either our quest for God or our musings about God's will, God's plan, God's *anything*. It just isn't the done thing, as the British would say, to even mention God's name.

This cultural embarrassment, however, intensifies one of the greatest hungers in ourselves and may explain, in part, the enormous "spiritual non-events" that plague us individually and collectively. Many of us are familiar with St. Augustine's impassioned prayer after a life of dissolution: "You have made us for Yourself, O God, and our hearts can find no rest until they rest in You." In our own time, the song "Is That All There Is?" echoes another side of the same restlessness, a feeling each of us has experienced when we actually acquire the object of our desire— and it just isn't enough.

On a recent spiritual retreat, a group of women from various professions came for the prayer and solitude that the rural facilities offered. One by one, before the weekend silence began, each woman shared her reasons for coming, and always the reasons sounded a similar note: They longed for peace; they felt that something was missing; they experienced their lives as too frantic and overcommitted; and mostly they felt a profound need for the presence of God. In some of us, that need is closer to the surface and is thus more easily articulated. But for many, though the need is real, it struggles to be expressed. Whether or not we are conscious of the need, however, at some level many of us imagine that we will find some spiritual union, and when we perceive that is missing, the sadness can be acute.

THE IDEAL ME, THE IDEAL I

At what point do we give up our dreams of becoming thin, healthy, orgasmic, intellectually and emotionally competent, or spiritually in tune with the highest part of ourselves? While letting go has its value, as we've noted, giving up is another issue altogether, implying defeat and being routed from the place of our dreams. We've seen this in the faces of men who told us they weren't really respected at work or particularly loved by their children. And we've watched too often as the dreams of older women seem to disappear in the mist of advancing years.

But Carolyn Heilbrun, an advocate for the older woman, maintains that it is never too late to recapture our dreams of becoming. She urges older women, who often feel invisible, to "make noise, to be courageous, to become unpopular." For she is convinced that:

> Baby boomers, notorious for their worship of youthfulness and beauty, and now soon to enter the circle of invisibility, need to know that instead of invisibility we have a new opportunity for effectiveness. [In fact] few women think of old age and power as compatible. . . . A door is closing behind us and we turn sorrowfully to watch it close and do not discover until we are wrenched away, the one opening ahead. Too few of us ask as Adrienne Rich does: "I'm calling you up tonight/as I might call up a friend as I might call up a ghost/ to ask what you intend to do/with the rest of your life?"[5]

To see doors opening for ourselves, when our own culture and expectations would see them closed, compels us to revisit the issue of who we really are. Heilbrun echoes this need to revisit and integrate the various aspects of our past and present lives, particularly as it relates to older adults.

> *The elder faces the task of bringing identity . . . into balance by seeking to make sense of the self that has lived through many decades, that lives in the present, and that will continue to live in the indeterminate future.*[6]

This need to revise our sense of self is not limited to the elderly, however. Psychologist Carol Ryff conducted a study of how different age groups compared themselves to their ideal selves and concluded that people's "self-evaluative horizons" continue to shift throughout their lives but change somewhat in perspective. The young adults in her study, for example, reported great strides in themselves since their adolescence and held high hopes for their futures. Theirs were the stories of unleashed expectations, often untempered by experience, whether triumphant or disappointing. The middle-aged adults also shared reports of self-improvement from the past to the present, and on most aspects of well-being they foresaw continuing progress, albeit at a lower level, in the years ahead. In contrast, the oldest adults saw themselves as holding steady, relative to the past, and the future looked more ominous to them. On the brighter side, however, these older individuals were also more accepting of themselves than the younger two groups. Thus, it appears that in later life, our ideal self can be more congruent with our real self, that individual "with whom one has become an accustomed traveler."[7]

It's clear then that making sense of our past and present selves is vital to all adults, regardless of age. Further, in order to realize our best dreams for ourselves, we must come to terms with our perceived errors and omissions, wrong turns and thoughtless gestures, and all our mistakes both public and private—and all our non-events as well. Only then can we find peace in the present and delight and hope in the future.

LEGACY—OUR ONCE AND FUTURE GIFT

But how can we address the discrepancies between our present and ideal selves? One way is to "take on a measure of a new identity as a fledgling ancestor, a progenitor of the next generations," a concept that illustrates the intimate connection between the dreams of self and legacy, our natural longing to be remembered or to know that our life has had meaning. In one sense, many adults may reason, if *I* didn't get it right, at least I can leave behind my values, my wisdom, my artistic and professional creations, my material wealth, and so on. In fact, much like the instinct that leads us to create a family, legacy involves an empathy and concern that cause us to "bequeath" to the next generation those qualities and gifts that we believe to be our best.

In *Vital Involvement in Old Age*, the authors revisit Erik Erikson's original conceptualization of the inner and outer conflicts that individuals resolve over the course of a life. Only this time, the concepts are applied to older adults. One theory long held by Erikson is that adults must wrestle with the issues of generativity versus self-absorption. For mature adults, the authors reassert, this means "a set of vital involvements in life's generative activities . . . in which one can learn to take care of what one truly cares for." In fact, the very acts of nurturing and sustaining others become the essence of generativity. For this capacity:

> *Incorporates care for the present with concern for the future—for today's younger generations in their futures, for generations not yet born, and for the survival of the world as a whole. It contributes to the sense of immortality that becomes so important in the individual's struggle to transcend realistic despair as the end of life approaches, inevitably.*[8]

Striving to transcend our own desires and attend more selflessly to others is also tucked into our dream of self. For apart from our attempts at physical, intellectual, and emotional growth, we long to be adults for whom generativity and care for others play a central role.

Generativity is thus about both the present and the future and, according to psychologist Douglas Kimmel, can be defined as:

> *Having left one's mark by producing something that will outlive oneself in some way, usually through parenthood or in occupational achievement . . . in the present. If one is generative one can nurture others; [but] if one is self-absorbed, one feels that life has been meaningless.*[9]

The shift from our need for generativity in the present to its future implications became apparent as we spoke to older adults or those facing life-threatening illness. Often they described two needs:

- The need to transfer to the next generation some part of themselves that they believe to be vital—that is, values, traditions, memories, or material objects or goods.
- The need to "matter"—to feel appreciated, noticed, and depended upon.

Essentially, though, both needs are bound to our fervent hope that, when we are no longer here, it will have been important that once we were.

THE NEED TO TRANSFER

The caring that informs our dreams of legacy can, of course, take many forms. As psychologist Carol Ryff notes:

> *Caring embraces taking care of whatever one produces—children, of course, but also all that one does or makes or is part of. It*

*involves playing an active role in social institutions that create the
coherence of a given social structure at a given historical time. Not
to be in any way productive and participate in the social network
in which one lives and works and loves must result in stagna-
tion—a sense of the end of growth, both personally and as a member of the community and the greater polis.*

Thus, Ryff concludes that "our legacies to others may
include an object, idea, value, tradition, or just a memory that
lingers."[10]

At seventy-eight, Rose illustrates the need that some
adults have to bequeath objects to others.

*All my life I have had to worry about making ends meet. I do not
have enough money for myself and I feel terrible that I am unable to
help my two daughters and five grandchildren, who need money.
When I was a young bride I never worried. When my husband, a
carpenter, died at fifty I still did not worry. I thought that if I
worked hard and continued to be responsible I could live well in old
age and not always be afraid. That security never came and now I
have nothing of substance to leave the next generations.*

Because Rose's legacy non-event centered on not being
able to pass along something material, she feels diminished and
despairs that now she must look to them for economic support.
Similarly, another adult confided that he and his wife had
expected an inheritance, but found out they were not in his parents' will. He said that while it was a shock to plan on a certain
level of financial stability that was never there, the worst hurt
was knowing he hadn't been remembered by his parents.

Melody, a nurse's aide, hoped to bequeath a less tangible
legacy. All her adult life, she had struggled as a single parent to
make ends meet, working long hours during the day and devot-
ing her heart and energy each evening to her son. When asked if
there was anything she'd like to bequeath him, she admitted:

It is much more than money. I have been trying to teach my son how to live; I try to give him my strength. But I am afraid he does not know, or if he knows he just wants to hurt me by ignoring my values. Sometimes I wonder if maybe he hates me and this makes me very sad. I cannot rest easy when I think about the future.

Sophia's dream of legacy was more global. For years, she had worked for an organization that helped Vietnamese children come to the United States. But a month before she was scheduled to go to Vietnam to facilitate the children's release, she was operated on for breast cancer. Sophia felt somewhat responsible for the inability to continue her life's work. She had been neglecting her health and when she noticed a lump in her breast, she chose to ignore it for months. At first, she was both angry at herself and profoundly disappointed.

Sophia's legacy non-event began to change her life considerably. On the positive side, she began making her health a priority. On the negative side, Sophia said that she was "less admiring" of herself now that she couldn't help others. Her assumptions about herself as a contributor to society had changed and she began casting about for another way to make a contribution. For Sophia, as for each of the others we've cited, the sense of self was tied to her sense of making a difference through her actions—both today and in years to come.

Brian is a bachelor who ultimately needed to place his senile mother in a nursing home. Brian felt relieved, on the one hand, but was saddened because his mother had always been a difficult, contentious woman and now the dream that "someday she'll find what she needs to make her happy" is gone forever. Brian naturally mourns for his own non-event—never healing the relationship with his mother. But mostly, he told us, he mourns for his mother's non-event—coming to the end of a life that won't be joyfully recalled by the child she leaves behind.

We learned other aspects of legacy's complexity from Neil O'Farrell, hospice expert and volunteer. Over the course of many years, Neil has tended close to forty dying patients and heard their dreams and heartaches, as well as the various discomforts of adults at the end of life.

> *At the time of their death, these people are not concerned about leaving their name on a building. Some of them talk about their memories, as well as the rigors of living and, now, dying. And sometimes they grieve for the jobs, the kids, the opportunities not taken. But mostly, if at all, they grieve for lost love. A hospice volunteer is thus in a privileged position to hear these laments and, in the listening, to help the dying endow their life with meaning.*[11]

The need for meaning, however unconscious, ran through the story of Reverend Morris. As Neil recounted, the reverend was forced to flee his home in the South after a minor incident with a white man. When he eventually migrated to Washington, D.C., he opened a storefront ministry, distributing food and clothing to the poor and using this contact as a chance to preach the Gospel. But his dream of helping others was shattered when riots destroyed both his small operation and the community around it. The reverend became embittered by the experience, but at some level the need to preach persisted. Finally, as Neil reported:

> *Reverend Morris lay dying in a room where he could hear gunfire and ambulances—reminders of the violence that still persisted—and that's when he preached his final cycle of sermons to me. Though his wife and children cared for him, they were tired of listening. (Sometimes this is true with the dying, who are enfeebled and no longer taken seriously.) But in those final days of preaching, the reverend seemed to be integrating a lifetime of dreams and pouring them out to a virtual stranger. I also found the reverend needed to be engaged in one last love relationship, something that at the end was new and hopeful. By listening, I could help him give his life shape. By being there, I could take him at face value. That*

is, he could struggle for that time of integration when our best selves and our real selves mirror each other most closely.

Once again, self and legacy weave their intricate alliance.

THE NEED TO MATTER

Like the reverend, as adults are confronted with mortality (their own and those of people they love), they begin to ask some age-old questions: How do I want to be remembered? Will it matter when I am no longer here? Will it matter that I was here? What happened to my dreams? Or as Lenora reflected:

> *I worked, raised three children, cooked, cleaned, but did my life amount to anything? Did I matter? When I am gone, will anybody notice? I know my children and grandchildren will notice, but in the long run did I do anything really worthwhile enough to be remembered for? I think I put in a lot of time spinning wheels.*

When the dream of legacy is unfulfilled, there dawns a sense of despair that there is nothing to show for our lives. Sometimes that feeling is bound to a perceived absence of being immortalized. As Edwin, eighty-two, lamented: "I have no children, no grandchildren, no books—no tangible proof that I was ever here." At the end of his life, Edwin now fears that his life will go unnoticed because he seemingly has nothing to leave behind. In an existential sense, he tells us, it will be "as if I had never existed." To combat his sense of despair, Edwin reviewed his will and set up a scholarship fund for disadvantaged youth at his alma mater.

Still, Edwin's story is an eloquent plea that each of us feels: We quite simply need to know that we matter. "Mattering" refers to the beliefs people have, whether right or wrong, that they are important to someone else, that they are the object of

someone else's attention, and that others care about and appreciate them. Mattering was originally described by sociologist
Morris Rosenberg as "a motive—the feeling that others depend
on us, are interested in us, are concerned with our fate, or experience us as an ego-extension [which] exercises a powerful influence on our actions."[12] He discovered that adolescents who feel
they matter to others will be less likely to commit delinquent
acts. Rosenberg further suggested that those in retirement who
no longer feel they matter will have difficulty adjusting to their
new status.

Contrast these two cases. Angus, the founder of a major
company, described his shock after retirement when his phone
no longer rang. Not only was he not the elder statesman he
expected to be, he was mortified to discover that former colleagues no longer wanted to have lunch with him when he was
in town. John is an eighty-three-year-old who feels he does matter: He is on the board of a hospital, currently raising money for
a center for abused children. He goes out each night, and works
each day, with time for golf only once a week. As John happily
reports:

> I must say that a lot of people think I am silly at my age to be
> doing all these things, yet I see so many of my friends with nothing
> to do. I feel the hospital needs me, and my special friend, whom I go
> dancing with, needs me too.

Mattering, in fact, is a concept to which people of all
ages respond. We frequently hear such comments as, "My boss
only notices when I do not do well. If only she would show me
some positive recognition or appreciation." Or, "I always feel my
mother is on my back, never quite approving of what Larry and
I do."

One last story from Neil: It seems that one hospice
patient had been a dress designer whose dreams of success were
thwarted. Though Roger's designs were admired by his clientele,

when these same clients scaled the economic ladder, they invariably turned to better-known designers. At one time, this was a source of keen frustration, but our dreams change, as Neil reminded us, and Roger seemed to put these setbacks aside when he became ill with AIDS.

> Then Roger entered a kind of molting process of letting go of the unessential and holding on to something that was. The way this expressed itself was through this one recurrent dream: In the dream, Roger was always in a room with floor-to-ceiling shelves that were filled with glorious pottery and ceramics. All of the objects were on the shelves, save one—the last, most beautiful piece of all, which he held in his hand.

> In time, Roger came to realize that the objects in the dream represented all the important things he had done in his life, the jobs he had held, the dresses and clothes he had designed—and that each of these "things" was completed now and back on a shelf, finished and relinquished. But the last best piece was the essence of himself, that piece that would not be surrendered until the moment of death.

As Neil recalls, Roger held on, waiting for some last signal that his life had indeed had meaning and that it was time to let go.

> Somehow Roger needed a sense of closure, that would help him take the next step. I remember that I tucked Roger in that day, kissed him on the forehead, and told him, "You are loved, you'll be remembered, and you have lived a good life." As I left the house minutes after, Roger died.

In reflecting later, Neil told us: "I believe that the idea of legacy can be transformative. In wanting to make meaning of our lives, we can become our best selves. Roger couldn't let go until he knew his life had mattered."

CULTURE AND POLITICS:
THE LARGER LEGACIES

Legacy, of course, embraces more than individual stories. The legacy of women's lives as a whole, for example, demonstrates the importance of passing on certain traditions and accomplishments from one generation to another. The right to vote or the right to job and salary equity are not the legacy of any one woman, but that of countless vocal and courageous women. Yet even today, argues one writer, women inherit the legacy of an unfinished story and are bound to complete it further for the next generation. The authors of *Mother Daughter Revolution* raise a controversial subject when they discuss the political aspect of legacy. Raising a daughter is an extremely political act in this culture, they argue. Mothers have been placed in a no-win situation with their daughters: If they teach their daughters simply how to get along in a world that has been shaped by men and male desires, they are betraying their daughters' potential. But, they continue, if they do not, they are leaving their daughters adrift in a hostile world without survival strategies.[13]

Esther, a working mother in her fifties, is typical of many women who hold to the older legacy:

> *I keep reading and hearing about the woman's movement, and I don't care what they say. I know the truth that it is important to look feminine, to wear makeup and perfume, and to set your sights on finding the right man. That is the wisdom I leave [my daughter].*

Hearing Esther's comment, one activist moaned:

> *When will people like Esther learn that all we have to leave our daughters is the power to be themselves, to be in charge of their own lives, to present to the world the real person not made up with eye makeup and blush?*

It seems then that we have both our individual legacies to consider and the broader cultural, sexual, racial, or ethnic ones that we inherit and choose to bequeath—in whole or in part—to the next generation. Perhaps Amy Tan, author of *The Joy Luck Club*, describes the importance of legacy best when she has one mother urge her daughter to defy her controlling husband. In her impassioned plea, the mother admits that losing the husband would be scary for the daughter, but not as scary as losing herself.[14] So too with the dreams of legacy that we choose to bequeath: They're never scary if they are ours.

SELF AND LEGACY: A FINAL GLANCE

As we've seen in many of these stories, the need to bequeath something from our lives to the next generation, to feel that we have mattered, that in some way we've made a difference, is vital to our well-being. Sometimes these legacies include our material wealth, but more often than not we hope that our values, our traditions, the memories of our lives, and the best in ourselves will persist into the future. Thus, of all our non-events, of all our struggles and dreams, those of self and legacy may be among the most important. For as we strive to shape our best and various selves, our present *and* our futures intertwine.

Coping

at Last:

PART III

The Dream-

Reshaping

Process

6

Acknowledging the Lost Dream

... to say the very thing you really mean,

the whole of it, nothing more or less or

other than what you really mean; that's the

whole art and joy of words.

—C. S. LEWIS[1]

It's fairly obvious that a problem unrecognized is a problem that usually persists. That's why the first step in dealing with non-events is to acknowledge that a dream has not been fulfilled. We are all ingenious at denial when it comes to our own lives. "Maybe someday . . . " "If my boss would only leave . . . " "Perhaps I'd find the right mate if I were thinner, smarter, prettier, richer, more muscular . . . " But neither wishful thinking nor fantasy is a cure unless we daydream the *possible* and take steps to achieve it. In the meanwhile, no matter how painful at first, we need to take a closer look at a lost dream and concede that this particular dream, just as we'd imagined it, just isn't going to happen—now or maybe ever.

That first step won't be easy. But the decision to go on cannot occur until the loss is admitted into our consciousness. Unlike events, which can be evident and even overwhelming, non-events are more subtle and frequently silent. For this reason, acknowledging their presence is much more essential to retrieving a new dream and moving on.

Let's consider the case of Annetta, a woman in her early forties who for years has suffered from back pain. Sometimes it is under control, but all too often she misses work or social events because the pain is unbearable. Annetta has been to the usual round of doctors, and today her knowledge of painkillers, muscle relaxants, and antispasmodics rivals the *Physician's Desk Reference.* If only Annetta will look beneath the surface—well beneath—she will discover that her back pain comes in great part from two non-events: one at work, the other at home.

Annetta can easily pinpoint the obvious tensions (or "events") at work: too much to do, inefficient support staff, a critical boss. And at home, the scene is not too much different: a husband who doesn't carry his share of household responsibilities, children who demand a lot and don't really pitch in. Annetta has never understood the key to her problems, so the vicious cycle has continued. The heart of Annetta's distress? Lost dreams and loss of control.

In Louise L. Hay's compendium *Heal Your Body*, the author lists a host of ailments and their possible emotional causes.[2] In particular, she focuses on ailments of the spine and back. Though Hay's theories have not been scientifically substantiated, she is not alone in believing that some back pains in particular are related to feeling burdened ("Get off my back"), angry ("Back off, will you!"), and powerless ("No one will back me up"). It is important to remember that many bad backs are caused by factors other than emotional stress. However, in Annetta's case, she feels both burdened and powerless as a consequence of two broken dreams.

To begin with, Annetta had longed for a partner who would be a helpmate. When she and her husband were dating, Annetta had every reason to believe from his thoughtfulness and their long discussions that he would carry that sensitivity into the marriage. Unfortunately, like all too many women, especially working women, Annetta has ended up shouldering virtually all responsibility for the house and the childrearing. Even the concept of "shouldering" a burden relates directly to back pain. As Annetta conceded: "At home I'm responsible for almost everything. I carry it all."

Annetta has summed up not only her sense of being burdened but also the anguish of her lost dream: She had expected to have a companion, a helpmeet, a life's mate who would share all the daily chores of living, not just the comforts. And if she looked more closely at the situation, Annetta would make a surprising discovery: Even if her husband helped a little more and her children were somewhat more appreciative and responsible about their chores, even *then* Annetta would feel her discontent. For at the source of this back pain, and the accompanying anger and sadness, is not just a sense of being tired and overworked, but of being cheated and of having relinquished a major part of herself. For enmeshed in Annetta's emotions about her husband and children is a feeling, if not an acknowledgment, that her expectation of "family" has not been realized in the deepest sense. This is not without remedy, of course, but only if Annetta first recognizes the more fundamental loss of a dream.

In the work arena, Annetta faces another major disappointment. True, she works entirely too hard for the salary she receives; her hours are too long because there is only a part-time secretary to help her; and her boss rarely gives her the satisfaction of knowing she's done a good job. Each of these obstacles would be surmountable, however, if Annetta felt empowered. If Annetta were in the position of management that she felt entitled to, she would not feel so unfairly burdened. In fact, two years before, Annetta had all but been promised a promotion if certain requirements were met. Excited and hoping to advance in her career, Annetta worked overtime and took on extra projects only to have two colleagues promoted while she was passed over.

In a way, this career non-event is easier to identify than the one at home. But it too is painful, in part because it is so public. The fact that Annetta's back problems cause her to miss work raises further questions about her professional capability. So what is the answer for her, and for those who experience the stress of non-events? As we have indicated, there are many strategies to employ in the dream-reshaping process, but often essential to moving on is acknowledging our disappointment at the deepest level.

This initial step was ultimately helpful for Cara, whose expected marriage never took place:

My coping strategies at the beginning were to hope for the best, that things would be better tomorrow, that this was just a bad dream. I couldn't admit to myself or anyone else that Ray wouldn't change his mind. I'd been in this relationship for almost eight years and I kept hoping and hoping and hoping. When I finally accepted the fact that the relationship was going nowhere—and never would— I began to think differently about my life. Now my coping strategy is to think about what will make me happiest. I keep in mind that the only person who is going to watch out for me is me.

As Cara recognized, however, this shift in thinking was impossible until she acknowledged that this particular dream had faded.

Sometimes we experience a non-event as a result of *something* happening, and then too we need to acknowledge the loss of a dream. Consider Leo's situation. Childhood mumps made it impossible for him to be a biological father. Then he and his wife needed to care for his ailing father in their home, which made adopting a child impossible. In his case, two events had precluded the realization of his original dreams. Ultimately, Leo became the beloved "uncle" of many college kids who frequented his house. Born to be a dad of sorts, Leo emotionally adopted dozens of young people eventually—but not before he acknowledged that physically and logistically other routes of fatherhood were out. "You know how you can know something, but not *really* know it?" Leo asked. "When I finally *knew* I wouldn't be a dad, I actually began to feel some relief." That relief came from identifying a significant heartache and beginning to enjoy the long discussions, dinners, and even trips with kids who had made his house a regular watering hole. In the end, Leo was determined to seize some joy from his situation—and he did.

Public Versus Private Non-Events: Tell Us Where It Hurts

From the stories we've shared so far, it's clear that some non-events are more painful than others because they are on display. Dreams that involve achievement in this country tend to be measured by externals: the prestigious title, the large salary, the overt acknowledgments that go with performing well on the job. Thus, career non-events can be painfully public.

Other non-events are painful precisely because they are so private. No one knew the discomfort Nick felt when his colleagues swapped Little League stories. Because many couples decide not to have children, no one in his office suspected that Nick was longing to be a father, and that these tales from proud fathers were difficult for him to listen to.

It's useful to understand in which arena your own lost dream resides, because that knowledge can guide your solutions. If a non-event is private, you can choose to avoid situations that are disturbing (in Nick's case, the water cooler at certain times) and adopt a publicly neutral attitude. A public non-event, on the other hand, needs to be handled a little differently, since our perceived failures are open to scrutiny. That's when it is useful to try to make meaning of our non-events.

Making Meaning

To make meaning is to make sense of a situation that has baffled us with its unpredictability or thrown us into a panic or depression by its seeming finality. Personally, when we think of making meaning, we are reminded of the illuminated maps in shopping malls. First we look for the words "You are here." Without analyzing the cognitive wisdom of this move, we know instinctively that there's no going forward unless we know where we *are*.

Much of the time we go along in the roles that we fulfill (spouse, parent, professional, and so on), and as long as our lives continue with fairly predictable outcomes, we cruise on "automatic pilot." But what if one of our roles is threatened or one of our dreams is shattered? Then our minds need to make sense of the circumstance and reorder our perceptions.

Luis, who experienced a career non-event over the course of seven years, reported mounting anger as he was passed over for promotions—not once, but several times. First he blamed himself, then his "prejudiced" organization, and finally his boss. Luis kept ruminating about these lost opportunities, talking negatively about the organization, and presenting himself as a "loser." Though each of these explanations was inadequate by itself, this early time of accusation was Luis's attempt to find meaning in a trying situation. In the long run, he found that there was truth in each aspect of the problem: His boss *was* unreasonable, his company never really *had* promoted minorities in any meaningful way, and Luis himself had not been doing his best work for some time. His first attempts to make meaning, however, were not wasted. They gave him a structure for coping until he had carefully thought through the situation. In the long run, he perceived his predicament in a way that proved more fruitful, and this larger, more accurate "meaning" guided him to further growth.

Over time, however, he understood that no amount of resentment would change the structure of his company or the people with whom he worked. Luis also came to realize that blaming the system was unproductive. He was able to acknowledge that this particular job was a dead end—an admission that allowed him to explore the kind of position and company that would make him happy. Today, Luis has made some careful career moves that soon should lead to new employment.

It is in our very nature to organize our world, to have that "blessed rage for order" so wonderfully described by the poet Wallace Stevens.[3] We like patterns and routines in our lives and, if these are missing, we create them through schedules, timeclocks, bibliographies, tables of contents, paradigms, models, and endless lists and organizational devices. However we find this order and meaning, we also need a mental and emotional structure to explain our lost dreams and to help us find significance in the midst of chaos. This is where naming, telling your story, and using metaphors can help.

NAMING

In an educational film entitled "Rites of Renewal," one scene depicts a group of women discussing the difficulties of divorce.[4] When asked what helped them through this trying time, each woman selected an event that named or labeled her in a different, more positive way.

One woman reported the importance of opening her own bank account. Another talked about changing the lock on the front door, packing her husband's clothes, and driving to his hotel, where she dumped them ceremoniously in the lobby. Rather than using pejorative names like "divorcée" or even "ex-wife," each woman had found a new label for herself: account holder, free agent, unencumbered individual. It was important that they gave a name to their new state of being as separate individuals with power and confidence.

Similarly, when we leave a lost dream it is helpful to give ourselves new labels. Just as these women who had experienced events were urged to define themselves in terms of what they now *are*, as opposed to what they are *not*, so too should adults who encounter a non-event. Phrases like "a woman with options" and "a man with new direction" serve us much better as we begin a new phase of life.

However, sometimes it is necessary to give negative names to a situation before we can begin to see the positive side. Howard, head of a major government agency, once reported at a dinner party: "It's strange to get to an age where my former students are surpassing me." "You mean you feel rewarded," commented another guest, "proud that you have made a contribution to the next generation." "No," he countered, "I don't mean that at all. I mean I feel diminished, maybe even a little envious."

At first glance, Howard may have seemed ungenerous. In truth, he was being honest. The stunning success of two of his former students served to underscore that he hadn't really gone as far in his own career as he'd wished. Denying that fact would not have helped him in the least. Once he gave his discontent a name, however, Howard could decide to pursue even higher career ambitions or reinterpret the situation as had his dinner mate. Perhaps it was time to regard his students' success as a source of pride. But only in acknowledging this non-event of sorts, and labeling his negative feelings, could this government official move on with new energy.

For this reason, when we encounter our own non-events, we need to be careful of the names or labels we give them. While it is helpful to be honest when we name our *feelings*, the negative labeling of *ourselves* should not persist. For example, if a woman is unable to bear a child, she is simply that: unable to bear a child. But to call her "barren" or "childless" is to endow that woman with labels that can be unnecessarily destructive. Similarly, when we make a serious mistake at work or remain in a relationship too long, we can simply describe those as facts about what we have done or neglected to do. These facts, however, say nothing about who we *are*. Rather, in these instances, we are people who can learn from our errors, adults who discover what a difficult situation has to teach and who strive to perform better in the future. For names and labels should only help, not hurt us.

Jennifer knew all too well the importance of labels. A successful married woman, she had become pregnant by another man, with whom she was having an affair. At first she was pleased, believing that they would divorce their partners and marry. In fact, she herself divorced and chose to give birth to this baby. To her sorrow, however, the child's father never left his first wife. Jennifer found herself in a uniquely difficult situation and wrestled with feelings ranging from shame and grief to anger and despair. "I've gone on with my life, but it still would be helpful to discuss . . . not marrying this man and having a family together. I need the comfort of giving this situation a label, to talk without fear of being judged, or worse, of judging myself." Jennifer acknowledged that both her marriage and this relationship had been unsatisfactory in part. She had learned from the joys and sorrows of both, however, and was now the mother of a little boy. There was nothing shameful about any of those labels. Further, she could live with all the names in that story because they had been said out loud.

TELLING YOUR STORY

Anthony de Mello once noted that the shortest distance between a human being and the truth is a story.[5] Human beings have always loved stories. In prehistoric times, the cave dwellers knew a story's value, for this was how they recounted their hunts and exploits and the gathering of food. We also imagine that their stories helped make sense, however limited, of their universe. Today, anthropologists tell us that their rituals were based on stories, which gave each clan member a sense of belonging.

All children love to hear the story of when they were born. Our children, who were adopted, never grew weary of their own stories when they were little. "Tell me again about how you adopted me and you said, 'That's the most beautiful baby I ever saw,' and then you picked me up and . . . " For children who are adopted, the story of how they came to be part of their family has prime importance. Besides a ritual of reassurance, their story is one that they can repeat to other children. It becomes a standard plot that can be told repeatedly without dredging up distressing emotions.

In one sense, a story—whatever its length—is a protective device: It heads off rudeness at the pass. In another sense, it is a form of shorthand that spares us reliving a difficult situation when we have to re-create a story each time the issue of an event—or non-event—is raised. Tomas, for example, had found graduate school a personal disaster. Besides the drain on his modest resources, he discovered that the classes were too challenging for him and that his business sense, so lively and creative in the store he had managed, was no help when it came to understanding theory. However, when he acknowledged that he would never earn a graduate degree, Tomas was ashamed at first to tell his friends and parents. Accepting the truth within himself, Tomas decided that baring his soul would serve no purpose, and he created a "story" that he repeated to others with increasing ease: "I decided that I'm happier managing a well-run store, and to do that I don't need to shell out for graduate school." In part, this was true. And as for any other subtleties in this decision, well frankly, he felt it was no one's business. In a kiss-and-tell world, we need to remind ourselves that we do have a right to privacy and that telling all isn't always beneficial.

On the other hand, if we are close to people who deserve our trust, there are many excellent reasons for telling a more detailed story of a non-event. Roger Schank's book *Tell Me a Story* describes the value of storytelling this way:

> *We need to tell someone else a story that describes our experiences because the process of creating the story also creates the memory structure that will contain the gist of the story for the rest of our lives. Talking is remembering.*[6]

But why tell stories about non-events, especially when they often deal with losses we would rather forget? Schank raises the same "to tell or not to tell" question and concludes that it is better to tell. For the best way to rid ourselves of a negative memory is to compose the story, tell it to someone, and then lay it to rest. The size of the audience, however, will vary with the individual and the non-event.

A poignant segment on National Public Radio once reported on a magazine created by and for New York children in foster care. Entitled *Foster Care Youth United*, the publication is a testament to the benefits of telling our story. Each issue features children's and teenagers' heartbreaking accounts of abuse, neglect, indifference, and fear. But each story is also filled with courage, hope, and even gratitude. As they were interviewed on radio, invariably those first-time writers spoke of the value of telling the world their stories. For these young people, their non-events were tragically evident: no parents, no love, little respect, and often inadequate food or clothing. But they felt a power in speaking the unspeakable, and felt that speaking gave meaning to the stories of their lives. It also earned them the respect of their foster parents, the social workers in the system, and other children in foster care. Most of all, it increased their own self-respect and determination.

Finally, telling a story can help us proceed with new dreams. We've found that by framing the non-event in a story, we can look closely at what dream we really expected, examine how we reacted when we didn't obtain it, acknowledge how its absence is changing our lives, and then begin to imagine future scenarios. Robert Frost once called poetry "a momentary stay against confusion." A story can do that for a non-event—for a much, much longer time.

USING METAPHORS

Mental health counselors have known the value of metaphors for years. Freud's dream analysis theory is heavily based on metaphors, as are the theories of Jung and many other psychotherapists. That's because metaphors involve symbols, pictures, and examples that can teach a larger truth. Some therapists have even found that humorous metaphors can drive home a point more effectively. Wrote one therapist:

> *Metaphors can lighten a therapy session without minimizing the seriousness of the client's problems and make explanations easier to remember. For example, consider this quick joke: How many mental health counselors does it take to change a lightbulb? Answer: Only one, but it really has to want to be changed. This metaphor's point that change requires motivation is accomplished without the mental health counselor's delivering a lecture.*[7]

In his work in adult education, David Deshler suggests metaphor analysis as a vehicle for learning. He writes that "metaphors can assist us in reflecting on our personal, popular, cultural, and organizational socialization, and [help us understand] the way we perceive, think, decide, feel, and act upon our experience."[8]

When we compare ourselves and our situations to other realities, we often get a clearer picture of our situation. Linda was even galvanized to change her career because of such metaphor analysis.

For years, she had experienced the non-event of never being a full-time English instructor at her university. Finally, distressed with the salaries of the part-time instructors, Linda went to the acting chairman to negotiate a raise. When it was clear that the discussion was moving nowhere, Linda took the plunge. "A lot of the instructors feel like I do and are even considering looking elsewhere for work." "Let them!" was the chairman's abrupt answer. "Part-time instructors are fruit pickers who can be replaced at a moment's notice."

That did it. As Linda left the office in disgust, the phrase "fruit picker" went through her mind repeatedly. It was that metaphor which helped her acknowledge the futility of her situation and seek full-time employment elsewhere. Today she is a program director at an international organization. When friends expressed dismay at the brutality of the chairman's remark, Linda countered with: "But I'm *glad* it happened. If he had been kinder and more conciliatory, I might still be at the university, hoping for a raise and better treatment. As it was, that comparison to fruit pickers drove home the reality that I was being exploited, that my career would never take off. That metaphor changed my professional life."

As Linda's experience illustrates, metaphors refer to comparisons that people make between two realities of life. In doing so, they provide "concrete images that require us to find the threads of continuity and congruence between the metaphor and primary subject." In Deshler's work, he too talked to dissatisfied university employees—faculty members, administrators, and support staff. And what he found was not unlike the example Linda provided. The metaphors these employees used clearly expressed their "hunger for appreciation and recognition, professional survival, a sense of community, empathy." Like Linda, these adults found themselves in situations that they described with phrases like "slave labor," "shophands," "cattle," "industrial labor force," and "warm body counts." While these examples might seem to be an indictment of the university system, they're not intended to be. The point is that when we feel undervalued—and not infrequently that's in the workplace—the metaphors we use tell us a lot about our non-events. For Linda, the metaphor "fruit picker" said it all, and empowered her to leave an unrewarding job.

As we see them, metaphors "have the capacity to empower and emancipate." Listen to the metaphors that run through your own mind. Do some of these implied comparisons sound familiar? "My marriage is a wasteland." "This office is a cage, a trap, a prison." "My boyfriend is a leech." Sometimes you may even catch yourself humming a song; pay attention to the words, because these too may carry metaphors. And if "Heartbreak Hotel" or "Lonesome Street" crop up once too often, take notice!

7

Easing Your Non-Event Stress

I have never learned to underestimate

the capacity of the human mind and body

to regenerate—even when the prospects

seem most wretched.

—NORMAN COUSINS[1]

ny discussion of illness or stress might seem at first glance to be depressing. But we believe that the mind plays a crucial role in our healing and that as long as there's life there is hope. Any discussion of non-events entails a discussion of stress, for when nothing happens, everything may change and one fairly predictable result is physical or emotional discomfort—or both.

Most of us are familiar with such emotions as anger, guilt, and shame. But usually we ascribe these emotions—when we *do* make the association—to things that *happen*, to persons who vex us, to mounting bills and worries, to having too much to do. It's important, however, to attend to all our emotional reactions, because something else might be present. Or, more accurately, absent.

With non-events we don't feel so much overwhelmed (as when the world is too much with us and events are crowding in) as out of control and powerless. From this perceived helplessness may follow feelings of being angry at life, disappointed, irritable without apparent reason, frustrated, trapped, and without hope. And with all of these emotions may come attendant aches, pains, and illnesses.

So where should we look for relief? And how can we regain our peace of mind? As popular wisdom goes, first we must seek lost objects in the place where we've lost them. Emotions are such a place, for they are the surest indicators of where our problems lie. Then in the act of recognizing our feelings, we begin to experience their impact. And when we do, when we allow ourselves the discomfort of "uncomfortable" emotions, relief is possible and future changes more likely.

EMOTIONS AS SIGNALS

Emotions may serve as signals, neither bad nor good, but neutral pieces of information. Psychologist Richard Lazarus assigns these pieces to various categories, including:

1. Those that result from a goal being thwarted or blocked.
2. Those resulting from a goal being attained.
3. "Borderline emotions" that reflect some ambiguity about whether or not the goal has been reached.[2]

Of these three categories, the first and last, which deal with thwarted goals, are clearly relevant to non-events. But even in the second category, attaining a goal, we may experience the emotion of a non-event, in a letdown of sorts when a dream doesn't meet our expectations. According to Lazarus, the emotions that accompany these categories take their rightful place in understanding the impact of non-events. They include:

- *Anger:* A demeaning offense against me and mine.
- *Anxiety:* Facing uncertain, existential threat.
- *Fright:* Facing an immediate, concrete, and overwhelming physical danger.
- *Guilt:* Transgressing a moral imperative.
- *Shame:* Failing to live up to an ego-ideal.
- *Sadness:* Experiencing an irrevocable loss.
- *Envy:* Wanting what someone else has.
- *Jealousy:* Resenting a third party for loss or threat to another's affection.
- *Disgust:* Taking in or being too close to an indigestible object or idea.

- 🐛 *Happiness:* Making reasonable progress toward the realization of a goal.
- 🐛 *Pride:* Enhancing our ego-identity by taking credit for a valued object or achievement, either our own or that of someone or group with whom we identify.
- 🐛 *Relief:* Resulting from a distressing goal-incongruent condition that has changed for the better or gone away.
- 🐛 *Hope:* Fearing the worst but yearning for better.
- 🐛 *Love:* Desiring or participating in affection, usually but not necessarily reciprocated.
- 🐛 *Compassion:* Being moved by another's suffering and wanting to help.[3]

To this list we have added

- 🐛 *Apathy:* Being lethargic and uninterested in life events around us.

Emotions, like the rest of life, are rarely tidy and distinct. Anxiety may have elements of fear, pride elements of happiness, and so on. Still, the list can be helpful as we appraise our non-events. To illustrate, imagine that you are feeling anger, jealousy, guilt, shame, and anxiety—all related to not being promoted. Such powerful emotions may be sending clear signals that your current situation is insupportable and future promotions impossible. In that case, it might be time to rethink your job prospects. Conversely, if you are experiencing relief, hope, and happiness from news that a cyst is benign, that a layoff won't take place, enjoy the moment. As we think about our non-events, we need to ask ourselves what emotions are evoked. The answers, as we will see, enable us to seize and shape new dreams.

It's important to note, however, that a particular non-event isn't followed automatically by a specific emotion. The mother who was unable to leave money to her children at first felt guilt and sadness. And when she eventually had to depend on them for support, that sorrow turned to shame. But other adults in the same situation might react differently. One might envy her friends with money, while another might be enraged that her husband died without life insurance. Still another might be anxious for her own future. In each case, our response will be shaped by our appraisal of the situation.

Emotional reactions, then, help us to understand the significance of our non-events. At the same time, they increase our self-understanding, which in turn helps us to manage our lives more effectively. Emotions thus provide helpful indicators that can lead to larger resolutions.

ANGER

Carol Tavris, a social psychologist, agrees that anger, like our other emotions, is neither good nor bad. Rather it is a message that insists: "Pay attention to me. I don't like what you are doing. Restore my pride. You're in my way. Danger."[4]

When we perceive a non-event as our own fault, we may experience guilt, shame, envy, and sadness. But when our goals are thwarted by circumstances outside ourselves, our reactions can turn to anger. When Marta was denied entrance into a doctoral program, she was devastated, sad, and depressed. When she investigated the reasons for her rejection, however, she discovered the decision had been based on her grade point average (2.8) from a bachelor's degree earned twenty years earlier. Since that time she had raised three children, had taken courses as a special student, and had maintained a 4.0 average, including A's in statistics. But none of her life experience or her recent academic excellence had been taken into account. At first, Marta was furious, blaming herself for low grades. But eventually the anger helped clarify her thinking, and she realized that she wasn't to blame at all for this lost dream. Her anger was redirected from herself to the administration's antiquated policies. Her newfound outrage led her to protest the university's decision. Finally, after six long months of appeals, Marta was admitted.

ANXIETY

Years ago, W. H. Auden labeled his time as the "age of anxiety"—an era of disquiet when uncertainty kept people off-balance. If the years surrounding World War II were a source of anxiety, how much more so is a nuclear age in which increasing violence threatens our lives both as nations and individuals?

Psychologists tell us that to survive, we need to give shape to a confusing world, to interpret it in such a way that we can navigate its roads and corridors. Without the assurance of maps or guidelines, however, we feel anxious and uncertain of our next move. The same is true, of course, with non-events, except that we usually fail to relate any vague, persistent anxiety to unacknowledged losses in our lives. Anxiety deserves our attention, for it is one of the more obvious emotional indicators that an expectation has gone unmet.

Mark was a technician at a major research laboratory. For years, other technicians in his department had been promoted at the end of their fourth year, so Mark, after three years, had no obvious reason to fear that he wouldn't be moving up. "It's premature to worry," he thought at the time, but still the anxiety persisted. Something was amiss in the process, but he couldn't quite pinpoint what. All he knew was that nothing was happening, no one spoke to him about moving ahead, no memos landed in his box that signaled he was in the "pipeline." "In the workplace," Mark told us, "knowledge is definitely power, and the fact that I knew nothing about the next step in my career made me really anxious."

As time passed, Mark was afraid to ask his supervisor about any future promotion and so, to allay his mounting fear, he began sending out feelers to other companies. Around the time he was scheduled for an interview at another firm, the news came down to his department: Forty employees were being laid off and Mark was one of them. "It was a good thing I listened to my anxiety," he told us. "It kept me from the unemployment line." Because anxiety is such a strong, if indistinct, signal, it can be one of the clearest signs that something needs our attention. Sometimes that "something" is a dream deferred.

SHAME AND GUILT

Many adults confirmed that shame and guilt were tied to a sense of loss or "failure" in their lives. Guilt perhaps is easier to understand, in that it's generally connected to an action we did or didn't take. In a sense, guilt comes from crossing our own internalized barriers.[5] In the area of non-events, many adults who lose their jobs, for example, or who can't find employment, experience an overwhelming sense of guilt. They reason that if they had been more talented, more productive, more aggressive, and so on, they would now be safely settled in their careers.

Shame, on the other hand, generates a feeling of displeasure with our very selves. As author Susan Miller observes, behind the feeling of shame is a greater sense of loss, "the fear of contempt which, on an even deeper level of the unconscious, spells fear of abandonment, the death by emotional starvation."[6] This feeling is thus one of the most powerful, tormenting emotions we can experience since it goes right to the heart of our identity. To make matters worse, we often feel ashamed of feeling shame . . . and the unkindest cycle of all continues within us. We didn't start life shame-filled, nor did strangers teach us to feel shame, as therapist Gershen Kaufman observes. Yet shame is all too familiar to many adults and often seems to surface when expectations go unmet. In *Shame: The Power of Caring*, Kaufman writes of enabling clients to cope effectively with shame:

> *One way concerns the appropriate handling of the client's shame spirals. The therapist needs to enable the client to learn to recog-*

nize, intervene consciously and terminate that internal shame spi-
ral. Attempts at understanding the experience while it is spiraling
or snowballing only embroil one deeper into shame. Deliberately
focusing all of one's attention outside oneself by becoming visually
involved in the world breaks the shame spiral and allows those
feelings and thoughts to subside. Later, the precipitating cause can
be explored and understood with one aim: to enable the client to
intervene even sooner in the future.[7]

This is obviously sound advice when we are experiencing shame related to non-events. In those moments when the shame is most profound, we need to leave reflection for a while and busy ourselves with outside tasks. Understand the source of shame, we are told, but intervene early to prevent unnecessary pain. Kaufman's advice would seem to contradict the wisdom of allowing ourselves to feel our emotions. But sometimes we need to resist our emotions for a while and give our battered psyches a rest.

Occasionally, the same situation will evoke both guilt and shame. Susan, now forty, admitted that when she was twenty she'd never imagined facing middle age without a husband and child. She feels *ashamed* because she imagines her parents thinking, "What is the matter with Susan?" Her parents, unfortunately, were highly critical and had set impossibly high standards for their daughter. Though both her mother and father have mellowed with time, Susan has internalized their earlier disapproval and today feels she's lacking as a person. Further, she also feels *guilty* that she has not "done what I should have to get connected to a man. If I had behaved differently, it would have all worked out." Unhappily, old scripts and reasoning now add to her discontent. But without shame and guilt, Susan could easily create a full, more joyful life for herself. Recognizing the power of her emotions and understanding their source is a first key step to letting them go.

REGRET: SIMILAR BUT NOT MATCHING

We experience regret when we feel sorrow or remorse for our actions or omissions. The difference between regret and guilt is that while we may regret an action, we do not feel consumed by the feeling nor do we feel the need to atone or expiate our wrongdoing. Brad spoke of career-related regrets. For years, he had been on the fast track, moving from city to city and ever closer to head of his company. But when the opportunity came for the next big move to vice-president, he turned it down. Remaining in the same job (a non-event of his own choosing), Brad had feelings of regret. On the one hand, he was proud of his decision and felt he'd made the right one for his family; on the other, he wondered if he'd made the wrong decision for himself and wouldn't have another chance. A year later Brad was investigating a Ph.D. program in business management, exploring research and teaching as a related but alternative career. He was past his regrets but realized he needed another plan in case the company penalized him for not moving up.

Sylvia also spoke of regrets in her life. Though hardly life-altering for most people, her decision long ago not to buy paintings by artist Roy Lichtenstein has bothered her subsequently. She had known his wife and admired his paintings, which at the time were very inexpensive. Still, she was reluctant to trust her judgment.

Years later, Sylvia developed a strong interest in art and regretted her initial caution. Rather than dwell on her error, however, she used the regret as an opportunity to examine other actions. Sylvia acknowledges that she'd been fearful about many things, and that her decision had merely reflected more deep-seated issues. Being resourceful and self-directed, however, she used her regret to break some old habits.

SADNESS AND DEPRESSION

The acknowledgment that a dream might never be realized inevitably leads to a sense of sadness. But sadness is usually temporary, unlike depression, which is bound up with feeling that life is hopeless or worthless. In fact, depression is a composite of emotions and a more complex reaction to loss. Often we are sad when an event is delayed or its outcome uncertain. Depression, on the other hand, can mask anger or rage when we feel helpless to change a situation—ever. Our focus narrows when we are depressed and, like shame, the feelings can consume us. As a consequence, outside distractions may provide temporary relief. But for severe or persistent depression, counseling should be sought.

APATHY

When we are involved in a life's work and invested in people we love, life carries meaning and each day holds at least some pleasure. But what if the challenge is gone, when our investment in a relationship or activity has diminished, and joy and excitement are no longer present? Apathy is the ennui or listlessness that ensues when life seems tedious and we find ourselves disengaged from activities and people that formerly mattered.

At twenty, when Florence married a man twenty-six years older, their age difference seemed irrelevant. They had enjoyed their careers, each other, and raising two young sons. When Ben retired eight years ago, however, he asked Florence to give up her career so they could spend time traveling. Though only thirty-eight at the time, Florence agreed, and the next years were a round of trips and leisure activities. Today, she reports being bored. "I lack independence, the camaraderie of colleagues my own age, and professional fulfillment. Some days it's an effort to get out of bed." For about five years, Florence lived an external life of pleasing her husband and an internal life of apathy and depression. What makes her non-event even more painful is the realization that it is in her control. She could choose to work, but is afraid that if she "gets a life" for herself, the marriage will be destroyed.

Her husband also fears that his wife will be less devoted to him if she works outside the home. But fearing the dissolution of his marriage even more, Ben has gone with Florence for counseling to find more areas of compromise. As is often the case, a simple emotion—in this case persistent apathy—was the catalyst for significant change.

ENVY

Some adults experience envy related to non-events. Dorothy's dream was to build a house. Though she'd enjoyed renovating three previous houses and knew just what she wanted, her husband was completely opposed to the idea. Eventually Dorothy resigned herself, but struggled to control her envy of people who had achieved that goal.

Realizing a *new* dream can be the surest escape from the envy trap. As Martin exclaimed: "Once I had had enough money to buy a car, I was no longer sick with envy when I saw friends whose parents had bought them cars. But before that, I felt it was unfair that I had no money, no parents, no resource of my own. I was thirty before this happened."

RELIEF

Most non-events relate to losses, but occasionally "nothing" happening can generate enormous relief. We think of Emily, who was diagnosed with cancer and given six months to live. Twenty years later, she is alive and cancer-free. In the beginning, each clear CAT scan brought a huge sigh of relief. Though the sighs are less dramatic with each passing year, Emily continues to enjoy the comfort of her continued health. Similarly, with many companies downsizing, many employees wait in fear that they will be let go. When they miss the fatal cut, of course, enormous relief ensues.

A word about survivor's guilt and other related emotions: When we dodge any number of bullets in life, the relief *is* genuine, but other emotions can enter the mix as well. We may feel guilty for being uninjured, alive, not laid off, able to conceive, able to find a mate, and so on. Or we may experience postshock trauma. For example, if a loved one has survived a heart attack, she *and* we may still reel from the close call. For a while, sadness and grief may ensue as part of the emotional cleansing that follows a narrow miss or traumatic situation.

HOPE

Hope, in the words of Kierkegaard, is "the passion for the possible." It is also one of the most crucial ways in which individual non-events may differ from each other. Now in her seventies, Marie has two adult children whom she had expected would marry and give her grandchildren. Her older daughter, however, began to have severe emotional problems in her late teens and has been in and out of hospitals ever since. Marie's hope was challenged, but she held on to the belief that her younger daughter would have a child. Within a couple of years, the younger married and decided to remain childless.

Marie provides an example of the role that hope can play in our lives. When we are fairly certain an event will happen (the sun will rise tomorrow, I'll still have my job, my family will be intact), we have little need for hope. But as the certain becomes only the possible, hope becomes a "powerful ally." Hope, in fact, carried Marie until her younger daughter announced she didn't want children. At that point, her passion for the possible died and she became despondent.

Psychologist Rick Snyder contends that we have the

means to revive our hope, which has two "operational" components: "agency" and "pathways." Agency refers to the will or energy to achieve our goals; pathways means the ability to see many ways of attaining those goals. Snyder has also developed a twelve-item "Hope Scale," which differentiates "high-hope" from "low-hope" individuals. Not surprisingly, he found that "high-hope" people generate alternative pathways to solving problems, and that when "the going gets tough, the hopeful keep going." In his own practice, Snyder works with clients to bolster their sense of agency—if that is what is needed. If, on the other hand, the problem is with pathways, Snyder helps his clients to see more options.[8] In other words, we must *want* to change. Then we find ways to bring that change about.

LABELS: EASING WITH ACCURACY

Just as it's helpful to name our non-events, it's also useful to label our emotional reactions to them. Identifying our feelings can bring us relief, especially when those feelings have been uncomfortable and ambiguous. Labeling also enables us to discuss those feelings with others.

The danger, of course, is that we might mislabel our feelings and prolong the discomfort. That's because it's sometimes difficult to know what we're actually feeling. For example, some depression is really masked anger, and the label of depression only obscures the real problem. Alicia's continual depression, for example, turned out to be anger at her husband for his total preoccupation with his work—a fact that a therapist enabled her to see. Our emotional reactions may also relate as much to past losses and hurts as to those in the present. Tyler's shame at not being promoted, for example, was doubly painful because it unconsciously reminded him of never measuring up to his father's high standards.

When we are unable to accurately label and relabel reactions (for as time passes, our emotions will change), counseling or psychotherapy can be helpful. We are not suggesting that everyone needs therapy, merely that it's an important option when we are confused about our feelings and in need of a listener who can help us cope more effectively. But whether we seek professional guidance or engage in self-diagnosis, understanding our feelings is a boon to managing non-events.

A VIEW OF OUR OWN

Our personal reactions, of course, are formed by many sources, but ultimately our appraisal of a situation consists of evaluating its significance as it relates to our well-being. Or as Lazarus argues, our appraisal of a situation "provides the emotional heat in an encounter."[9] The intensity of that heat, however, will be determined by other factors. For example:

❧ *How invested am I in this non-event?*

Dorothy, our would-be house builder, was actually in the midst of three non-events: She wasn't building her dream house; she wasn't a grandmother, though all her friends were; and she didn't get the promotion she'd anticipated. Obviously, each of these non-events had different significance for her. But only Dorothy could determine which was the most important to her well-being and, therefore, the most troubling. To help her identify the most critical, Dorothy answered the following series of questions:

❧ *Who is responsible for my non-events?*

In the case of Dorothy's dream house, her husband was. As for not being a grandmother, Dorothy knew her children's life choices currently precluded that. And she blamed her plateau at work on her own lack of initiative.

❦ *What are my emotional reactions?*

Dorothy was now envious of others with wonderful houses; sad but hopeful about her status as grandmother; and bored and mildly depressed about her career.

❦ *What do I hope for the future?*

Dorothy had no hope at all of having her dream house; she still hoped to have grandchildren someday; and she had little hope of changing her career status.

These same questions could help Brad think about his decision not to be promoted and move his family to another state. Though this career non-event was of his making, in a sense, he had groomed himself for a CEO position for many years. Then family obligations influenced his decision to decline the promotion. Brad too might ask himself:

❦ *How invested am I in this non-event?*

Brad was very invested in his career, but he made a conscious decision to make family even more important than career.

❦ *Who is responsible for my non-event?*

Brad took full responsibility for his decision. He also knew if he had moved, the family friction would have been tremendous. In that sense, his wife and teenage son carried some of the responsibility.

❦ *What do I expect for the future?*

Brad decided to make two plans for the future. If the company came back to him in five years with a similar offer, he and his wife agreed he would take it. If the company started edging him out because he hadn't cooperated the first time, he'd go back to school for a doctorate in business and gain "status" another way.

🥄 *What are my emotional reactions?*

Brad felt several emotions—regret for what might have been, anger at his family for putting him in this position (though they hadn't really pressured him), and relief that the decision had been made.

These questions highlight the interaction between a non-event, our evaluation of it, and our subsequent emotional reactions. And the answers will give us more clarity about our situation, including an idea of whom we *blame* for our lost dream.

BLAME: ITS USE AND ABUSE

Either we hold ourselves responsible or we point the finger at others, including "society" (the all-purpose scapegoat), our families, our circumstances, our appearance, our intelligence, our friends, or our miserable luck of the draw. If blaming were productive, many of us would be total masters of our fate by now.

Unfortunately, as many adults learn to their sorrow, blame plays an especially deadly role in the area of personal relations. In *Long Day's Journey into Night*, Eugene O'Neill produced a theatrical example of characters who create menacing triangles that form and dissolve as the objects of blame are replaced. First the mother's addiction to morphine is the "fault" of one family member, then of another, and ultimately all the characters remain stuck in a psychological warp. At the same time, the mother regresses emotionally until, in her mind, she is once again a schoolgirl in an interval when life's choices lay before her. Meanwhile, blaming has all but torn the family apart.

Carol Tavris agrees that blame can be counterproductive:

> *In the final analysis, managing anger depends on taking responsibility for one's emotions and one's actions: on refusing the temptation, for instance, to remain stuck in blame and fury or silent resentment. Once anger [and blame] becomes a force to berate the nearest scapegoat instead of to change a bad situation, it loses its credibility and power.*[10]

Despite the dangers of blame, however, it may be useful in addressing the source of our problem. For example, if we blame ourselves for a non-event, we can work on our own habits and tendencies; if we blame society, we can become involved in social action; if we blame our supervisors, we can express ourselves to those individuals, and so on. Though blaming can keep us locked in a game of denial and finger pointing, it can also galvanize our energies, enabling us to better decide on a future course of action—*or* inaction.

Any emotion that keeps us stuck will keep us from reshaping our dreams. But rather than fight the feeling of blame, it may be useful to go with it *initially*—to use it to explore why we're feeling envious, angry, sad, anxious, or otherwise uncomfortable. We may then decide to seek a therapist, confront the person we blame, or simply let the feelings go and forge ahead to new goals.

GOOD GRIEF: IT COULD CHANGE YOUR LIFE

People's overall reaction to their non-events is similar to the grieving process. At the beginning, grief is more acute—when they realize, for example, that a marriage will never be satisfying, that a child will not be born, that the promotion has gone to someone else. That's when many seek outside support. Moreover, that early provision of support from friends, colleagues, family, or therapists proves crucial to regaining a sense of hope.

In time, many adults become more proactive in accepting responsibility and dealing with their circumstances. Some work on finding new meaning in the non-event, others accept their lot and focus on managing their reactions to loss, while others take positive action to change direction in their lives. These choices are not unlike the process that occurs after a loved one is lost.

While depression involves complex reactions to loss, grief actually represents the struggle to cope. Or as Lazarus observes:

> Grieving is the process of coming to terms with . . . loss, especially the loss of meaning. When grieving is successful, old and cherished meanings are retained and integrated with more serviceable new ones . . . more appropriate for the new life condition.[11]

Often the initial response to grief is one of shock and disbelief, which in time is followed by great sorrow. Eventually people search for meaning in this loss, however, after which there is usually a decision to proceed with life.

Of course, people feel grief for many losses other than those most commonly recognized as causing bereavement. When we leave familiar surroundings, for example, or change jobs or schools, divorce, or find that our relationships with others have changed, we may feel a grief that shocks us with its intensity. So too with non-events. In an analysis of coping strategies that were most helpful to adults dealing with non-events, grief was mentioned as a major means of coping.[12] For many people then (except those with positive non-events), grief will be an essential first step to pursuing new dreams.

Still, grieving for a lost dream may be difficult because it is so private. Our friends bring soup and sympathy when we're sick or a loved one dies. But who brings either when you don't get the promotion? When your baby is never conceived? When the book goes unpublished, the doctorate unfinished, the relationship unfulfilled?

Author Kenneth J. Doka describes disenfranchised grief—a special kind of grief that:

> Is not or cannot be openly acknowledged, publicly mourned, or socially supported. The concept of disenfranchised grief recognizes that societies have sets of norms—in effect "grieving rules"—that attempt to specify who, when, where, how, how long, and for whom people should grieve.[13]

As Doka observes, these rules may even extend to personnel policies in which three days of bereavement leave from work may be granted for a parent or sibling, and five days for a spouse or child. The message is that "society defines who has a legitimate right to grieve, and these definitions of right correspond to relationships, primarily familial, that are socially recognized and sanctioned."[14]

How does this apply to non-events? Doka cites three reasons adults may experience disenfranchised grief: The relationship is not recognized; the loss is not recognized; the griever is not recognized. Adults who mourn their non-events may find themselves in similar circumstances. The dilemma then is that if the loss of a loved one—or dream—weren't grief enough, the loss of recognition causes the grief to be intensified. The abundance of research on "normal" bereavement chronicles the many feelings of numbness, anger, sadness, depression, loneliness, guilt, hopelessness, and depression. But when solace, support, and understanding are absent, these emotions can be even stronger. That is because an emotion denied can be an emotion that will return with even greater force. Fortunately, in our exploration of non-events, we encountered both the necessity for grief and adults' considerable progress when they let themselves truly feel their sorrow.

Cara, whose expected marriage never took place, said: "My coping strategies at the beginning were to hope for the best ... that this was just a bad dream. ... Now my coping strategy is to think about what will make me happiest."

It is important to realize that holding on to anger or blaming can be unproductive. Frequently, grieving can move us past the stage of holding ourselves and others "accountable."

EXPRESSING THE EMOTIONS OF GRIEF

While change in our lives can evoke grief for relationships, roles, and routines that are left behind, out-and-out grief is something more profound. Sometimes a deep sigh is sufficient and on we go. But if we've invested heavily in a person, a career, or a dream, the loss will be much keener. Not surprisingly, we found that there's no one right way to mourn a loss. But those who cried and *directly* mourned their lost dreams were those able to heal the hurt more fully. On the other hand, respondents who denied their pain, blamed others for their misfortune, or stayed stuck in hopeless situations were the least likely to reshape their dreams and move on.

NON-EVENTS: WHEN DREAMS ARE FULFILLED!

Occasionally, in the recalcitrance of human nature, we even grieve when our dreams are fulfilled. One respondent, Larry, spoke earnestly of the day he bought a partnership in a gas station. "I had worked toward that day for four years, giving up time, freedom, money, and even relationships. Owning my own business was the dream of a lifetime, and when I achieved it I expected to feel euphoric. Instead, it was a letdown, but I'm not sure why."

Larry's experience is not unique. For now and then, a non-event takes the form of relief *not* experienced, emotions *not* deeply felt. In Larry's case, he was sad that this particular journey had ended and that he didn't experience the anticipated elation. His grief was not in losing, but in attaining his dream.

Many psychologists argue that grief is the inevitable response to any loss, even when that "loss" refers to a positive ending like finally earning a degree. All change, in fact, involves loss as well as new possibilities. In Larry's case, he had contradictory impulses—a yearning for the thrill of anticipation itself, coupled with a longing to realize his dream. As Larry learned, the management of this ambivalence was essential to better handling his life transitions.

Of course, non-events by definition involve both change and loss. For if we seek to reshape our lost dreams, we risk *more* loss by changing the status quo. A catch-22 situation? Not if we recognize that grieving is part of any change, and often the herald of better things to come.

OTHER NON-EVENT RELIEF

Beyond our grieving, where can we turn for relief? In our work with many adults who coped with loss most effectively, we found that some of their most productive stress-reduction strategies were seeking support, journal writing, faith, and humor.

SEEKING SUPPORT

Because some of our non-events are so private, many adults remain silent about dreams that got lost. Others wonder: To whom can I say the unsayable? To a therapist? A friend? A bartender? A barber? Someone in my family? If we're lucky, there's someone in our lives who will hear and understand what we define as the worst parts of us. It's been said that most people tend to compare the *inside* of themselves with the *outside* of other people. Clearly, we're bound to lose in a comparison that allows our own private fears and self-criticism to share the stage with the shining exteriors of others. So to whom can we turn if a non-event has us feeling inadequate or miserable? Each of us needs to be championed by our own selves. But sometimes it gets a little lonely and we need a dash of affirmation, assistance, or just plain affection.

We know that no one person can meet all our needs, so it helps to be clear about *what* we need. If living with a non-event has you longing for levity, call a funny friend. If financial straits are the result of career difficulties, look for a source that can help you budget or tide you over with a loan. Sometimes we only need someone to listen, to understand what we're feeling, and then we can marshal the energy to take action. Only *you* know what you need, and you'll usually know who can provide it.

David was fortunate to know what was bothering him and to have a friend in whom he could confide. A middle-aged executive, successful by anyone's standards, he often spent time with friends who were even more successful. In fact, David was in a lunch group with several men who were celebrities, which began to feed his private concerns about his own success. David's wife, children, and relatives admired him greatly, calling him a "big shot" and admiring his career moves and "important" friends. But David became consumed with feeling unsuccessful. First he tried telling himself that he was being foolish, that he had achieved a great deal for a man of his age, of *any* age. He then thought of talking to his wife, but felt it would be unmanly to admit to feelings of inadequacy.

Then one summer evening, David sat by the pool with his oldest friend from college. The two men had not seen each other for twenty years, but they had had a history of emotional closeness that dated back to their fraternity days. So David found himself telling his friend about these "ridiculous" feelings and talking about all the things that had *not* happened to him, events that he'd expected over time. Fortunately David could pinpoint his non-events: He'd expected to be made president of his firm; he'd expected to have his book be a bestseller; and he'd expected to be more central to his friends who were celebrities. And David's friend just listened. He didn't offer solutions or advice, but he reflected that it must be difficult when one's frame of reference is a group of celebrities instead of just "ordinary" successful men and women.

David was both relieved and comforted by this exchange and soon found, from this one brief talk on a summer night, that much of his dissatisfaction began to dissipate. After that, when he was tempted to play the old comparison game again, David recalled his friend's kind words and they gave him the distance to look at his situation more clearly.

Events—bad and good—invite their own response. But when a non-event is eating us, no one will know unless we tell them. And when we do? Or when others confide in *us*? We can seek various kinds of support for ourselves or for others.

JOURNAL WRITING

Sometimes there is no friend to share with, no therapist we can afford, no family member to whom we can spill our feelings. What safer place than a journal, then, to pour out our concerns? Though David was fortunate to have his poolside conversation, sometimes it's humiliating to tell a friend about our envy, our insecurities, our dreams that haven't come true. That's when a blank piece of paper—for our eyes only—can allow us to present ourselves without censorship.

Lauren, a woman in her forties, described her journal as a safety valve during a difficult transitional time. Though attractive, successful, and delightful to be around, Lauren had a list of non-events that left her deeply discouraged. She was the first woman executive in a major corporation. Because in each preceding job she had made her mark, worked well with colleagues, and accomplished her tasks creatively, Lauren had every expectation that she would be successful in this job too. Full of hope, she assumed her new leadership role.

After three years, however, she felt like a failure. Her staff was in disarray and her divisional profits down. Lauren expected to be fired, but debated whether to resign first. Externally, she still dressed and played the part of successful executive. But inwardly, she felt almost adolescent again, continually self-absorbed and unable to confide her panic to anyone.

Then she read an article about journal writing that claimed that the process could reduce stress and physical complaints, and even bolster the immune system. Lauren immediately started keeping her own diary. In it she explored why the corporation had hired her, why things had gone downhill, what her role in the disaster was, and how she could regain confidence and deal with this lack of success. Today Lauren still wonders if she should stay with her company, but her job is stable for now and the constant sense of panic has declined. She also still keeps a journal, which has clarified many things for her.

FAITH

Over the years, research on how adults cope with transitions has reflected their increasing reliance on a force or power greater than themselves. This hunger for things beyond us is often most manifest when material or human comfort proves inadequate. As Rabbi Harold Kushner notes:

> Our souls are not hungry for fame, comfort, wealth, or power. Those rewards create almost as many problems as they solve. Our souls are hungry for meaning, for the sense that we have figured out how to live so that our lives matter, so that the world will be at least a little bit different for our having passed through it.[15]

When non-events threaten our equilibrium, solace can be sought in spiritual ways, and that search for meaning may redirect our energy. One man told us that he'd turned to Buddhism to help him relinquish anger; another attended Adult Children of Alcoholics meetings (which uses the same Twelve Steps as Alcoholics Anonymous) to help him handle never reconciling with an alcoholic father. Still others have confided that their difficulties have reminded them of their mortality. "Who wants to be reminded?" one woman asked us. "But when I am, I admit that it makes each day more special." Some of our subjects reported that their greatest resource was going to church. Others said it was their faith in a Supreme Being, not a church, that carried them through.

One respondent found that God and gambling were the right combination! At fifty-nine, Ilene had suffered several personal losses, felt tired and old, and regarded her life as one big non-event. She even considered suicide. Then her son drove her to Las Vegas. Reported Ilene in her interview with us: "Two days at the tables changed my perspective. That plus religion. Now, I'm not a fanatic, but these days religion is always with me." It seems that one took her *out* of herself and the other *beyond* herself.

We should also mention an unlikely *New York Times* article entitled "Therapists See Religion as Aid, Not Illusion." According to recent research, there's been a marked change in how psychology regards religion.

> *While Freud dismissed religion as little more than a neurotic illusion, the emerging wisdom in psychology is that at least some varieties of religious experience are beneficial for mental health. The result is that growing numbers of psychologists are finding religion, if not in their personal lives, at least in their data. What was once at best an unfashionable topic in psychology has been born again as a respectable focus for scientific research.*[16]

Finally, there may be comfort simply in prayer, in whatever form that prayer may take. It may be a walk in the woods, solitude at home, reading an inspirational book, or attending a religious service. Prayer for each person is an intensely personal activity, but when it lifts our hearts beyond grieving, fear, and pain to an all-comforting Presence, it's surely an act that is holy.

HUMOR

Sometimes, we may need to laugh our way back to health or, at the least, find humor in our situation. The following example of one woman's humor is based on an event that *created* a non-event—a phenomenon, as we've noted, that is not uncommon. In early adulthood, Krista remembers being wheeled in for the surgery that ended her childbearing chances forever. Because this occurred at a university hospital, several residents from around the world were in the operating room to observe the procedure. Right before the anesthesia was administered, the introductions were made across the table. "This is Dr. Woo from Beijing and Dr. Collins from Pittsburgh and . . . " The hand-shaking continued over Krista's abdomen, until finally, when there was a break in the pleasantries, a voice piped up from below: "And I'm Krista, the patient—in case you're wondering why you're gathered here today." With a flash of humor, Krista had deflected the doctors' rudeness and interjected herself into the arena. In the years that followed, as Krista faced the non-event aftermath of that day, her humor and assertiveness have served her well.

Joshua threw himself a party for the book that never got published. He enjoyed the ritual and saw it as a humorous way to deflect his feelings of defeat. Similarly, Agnes gave herself a divorce party when her marriage of many years failed to survive. From all reports, it was a hilarious occasion.

Humor can be a real boon during difficult times. It is also physically therapeutic. As Bernie Siegel describes it, hearty laughter "produces complete, relaxed action of the diaphragm, exercising the lungs, increasing the blood's oxygen level, and gently toning the entire cardiovascular system."[17]

Norman Cousins once confirmed this theory through his self-devised program to recover from serious illness.

> *Nothing is less funny than being flat on your back with all the bones in your spine and joints hurting. A systematic program was indicated. A good place to begin, I thought, was with amusing movies. Allen Funt, producer of the spoofing television program "Candid Camera," sent films of his classics, along with a motion-picture projector. The nurse was instructed in its use. We were even able to get our hands on some old Marx Brothers films. We pulled down the blinds and turned on the machine.*

> *It worked. I made the joyous discovery that ten minutes of genuine belly laughter had an anesthetic effect and would give me at least two hours of pain-free sleep.*[18]

With humor, we also increase our self-confidence by distancing ourselves from the problem. Is humor a temporary solution at best? Possibly, but coping implies a *continuum* of strategies, with each one allowing us more room for hope.

STRESS-REDUCTION TECHNIQUES: A POTPOURRI

Besides journal writing and seeking outside support, there are other ways to relieve the physical and emotional effects of stress. We can walk, run, jog, skip rope, swim, or practice karate. We can also lift weights, ski, dance, or simply walk regularly. Whatever method of exercise we choose, our body's natural mood elevators, called endorphins, are released when we exercise. A positive change in mood, of course, goes far in relieving the stress of non-events.

Some people prefer relaxation techniques, such as meditation, yoga, or deep breathing, all excellent ways to "let go" of distress. Others enjoy the benefits of massage—another natural technique that can restore us to a good and comforted sense of ourselves. As one woman reported, "I love to be touched and when I'm without a partner, as I am right now, massage is a safe and gentle way to feel centered in myself."

Whether we employ massage, acupuncture, yoga, meditation, walking, or deep breathing, the important point is to find something that works—strategies that relieve the tension and distract us from focusing *unproductively* on the hurt. Restoring balance should be the goal of any stress-reduction technique, but especially the ones that help us recover from a non-event. Thus restored, we can better face and shape the future.

Here's how one woman tailored stress reduction to meet her particular needs. Barbara's non-event, not getting into graduate school, changed her life dramatically.

> *Through the spring, when my peers were getting acceptances and job offers, I changed from supportive companion to jealous friend. I had no direction, I started skipping my undergraduate classes, lying out in the sun, partying even when I didn't feel like it. I gave up on my dream of being a physical therapist and thought I was dumb. Though I knew I would apply to other schools, eventually, that first rejection hurt me a lot. Finally, I turned to exercise for relief. I ran, I participated in an aerobics class, and I found that I could cope with my feelings much better.*

Like Barbara, we too can strive each day to ease our emotional and physical discomforts. Exercise in particular can give us a sense of *motion* when a non-event seems to have us stalled.

In Praise of Way Stations

Most of the strategies we've described are merely temporary measures, way stations, so to speak, where we stop for relief and refueling. They may not remedy the source of the problem, but understanding our emotions, seeking support, exercising, and so on will help us in the present. Much as doctors must anesthetize a painful area before they can suture or operate, we need to relieve the worst of our anguish before choosing a more promising future. As we've discovered, feeling our own emotions and finding appropriate outlets for stress are vital to relief. Thus supported, we are able to move on.

8

Shifting the Focus to Hope

Hope is the thing with feathers

    That perches in the soul

And sings the tune without words,

    And never stops at all.

—EMILY DICKINSON[1]

We need to shift the way we look at a non-event, to adjust the lens of our perceptions so that we can change our view of lost dreams. In naming our lost dreams and easing our secret losses, we take just the first steps in a process that should become increasingly hopeful. That's where refocusing becomes an essential aspect of moving on. For refocusing serves as a link between the past and the future, as a bridge between endings and commencements.

SOME VIEWS OF THE BRIDGE

Just as we know there is a process of entering a new role or realized dream (becoming a new parent, starting a new job), there is a process of "exiting," of leaving the familiar and striking out into new terrain. The process, of course, can be an unpredictable, even bumpy one, but leavetaking in life is just as essential as new beginnings.

ON THE ROAD AGAIN

Several researchers, including transition expert William Bridges, suggest a structure for regarding this leavetaking process. Every beginning begins with an ending, which in turn becomes the *first* phase of a transition. For Bridges, the second phase is "a time of lostness and emptiness before 'life' resumes an intelligible pattern and direction."[2] And the third phase signals the next beginning. But what if we get stuck on the bridge? If the lostness and emptiness persist because there seems no end in sight? The benefit of refocusing is that it provides a mechanism for moving forward on the bridge.

To understand how life's traffic gets stuck on its bridges—to continue the metaphor—let's consider an example of a retirement non-event. Harry had looked forward to retiring for many years. His plan was to "sleep past 6:00 A.M." and to travel and spend time with his wife, Kim. In the interim, Harry and Kim took trips to Florida to locate a place to settle when they retired, and they began to invest time, money, and imagination in their new anticipated life. They even went so far as to buy a small condo. Their habits back home also began to change in subtle ways. Harry went out less frequently with his friends and Kim grew less involved with the other wives at Harry's work. In short, they were appropriately pulling back from their present roles and anticipating the next step in their lives.

As the year for retirement approached, however, Harry found that he couldn't afford to leave his job. Suddenly Kim's mother needed nursing care, and the couple's economic resources were drained. From the day of her initial illness, Kim's mother lived another seven years. By the time she died, Harry and Kim had long been living a retirement non-event. It was clear to them that they needed to reexamine their lives very closely. Somewhere along the way, the Florida dream had died. Retirement, of course, was still a certainty, but where? And how? It was clear that both Harry and his wife had experienced an ending, and that now they felt paralyzed by their uncertainty. If their life was to resume its hope and purpose, they needed to shift the old expectations of retirement (not lower them) and to imagine their future in another way.

But the process of shifting focus isn't easy. As Bridges laments: "Considering that we have to deal with endings all our lives, most of us handle them very badly."[3] This is in part because we misunderstand our endings and confuse them with finality. In Harry's case, the ending of the Florida dream, however wonderful the plan, was but the beginning of something else. In fact, Harry and Kim were only able to pull themselves out of a vague despair when they looked more closely at retirement. These later years did not equal "Florida," though to Harry and Kim they had for a long time. The couple needed to rethink their idea of retirement, which had originally included travel, leisure, and time together. Eventually they decided to sell both their Florida condo and their permanent home and settle in a retirement community where modest maintenance and grounds fees would free them to travel and pursue other interests. The best part of this arrangement, reports Harry, is that with this revised dream, they've kept many of their old friends. Clearly, for Harry and Kim, the turning point came when they shifted their focus from the trappings of the old dream to the essence of the dream itself.

Understandably, changing roles and dreams can cause panic. That's because we identify so closely with them that a radical shift can be very disorienting. This is where a change in lens is essential. Part of this shift is a psychological leavetaking, relinquishing aspects of our "old" selves that no longer fit the new reality. So too with non-events. The loss of the dream of marriage, bearing a child, entering a meaningful career, being promoted, staying in familiar surroundings, maintaining reasonable health—each of these deep disappointments can pry us loose from our former selves and leave us bereft of the contexts in which we had known ourselves. At this point, refocusing becomes essential as we face our lost hopes and cast about for new ones.

Talia, a woman in her late thirties, was indeed feeling bereft in her stalled career. From the year of her first management position, Talia had frequented all the right business conventions, networked in her field, and enjoyed the companionship of other midlevel managers. In time, however, some of the managers moved on to other circles as they were promoted at their various companies. During these middle years of her career, Talia had perceived herself as a "woman on the way up," but with the passage of time, her own contexts and the people in them had shifted. Unfortunately, Talia's self-assumptions had remained the same. Feeling trapped, she only knew she was miserable in the present and could see no reasonable exit from her situation. Eventually, when a slow despair began to drain her energy, clouding her workdays and weekends, it was time to break apart some old beliefs and refocus her gaze.

A rather simple parallel to that breaking apart was apparent to one of the authors when she attended a concert performance. Straining to see tenor José Carreras through her opera glasses, Susan found it necessary to break apart the old image— adjusted for other eyes at another distance—before she could focus clearly on Carreras. The breaking apart in life can be distressing, but the metaphor holds. As with opera glasses, we need faith that we *can* fine-tune our perceptions and that a new, and even better, picture will eventually come into focus. Until such time, however, we seem, like Talia, to be free floating in a kind of limbo.

LIMBO

By definition, uncertainty is unsettling. Think of the uncertainty of adolescence, when as teenagers many of us agonized waiting to be asked to the prom; when we lived in dread of those report cards that could determine our social fate for the next grading period; and when we and our friends all but camped by the mailbox awaiting the announcement of a larger fate from the colleges of our choice. This anxious anticipation, of course, is most difficult because it implies that our life's direction is in someone else's hands. Not so with refocusing. While we may have to wait for certain events or non-events to play themselves out, we can and *must* choose how we wish to perceive that wait. Again Bridges counsels patience in this period that he labels the "neutral zone": "We need not be defensive about this apparently unproductive time-out at turning points in our lives, for the neutral zone is meant to be a moratorium from the conventional activity of our everyday existence."[4] The neutral zone, of course, can be wisely and wonderfully used. Some of our interviewees have used this time of being "in between" to pull back from daily obligations and take a variety of "vacations" from life. This might include a weekend away, a short leave of absence from work, a long afternoon walk, or even scheduled, periodic quiet times each day. Each of these retreats provides a time to honor the suspension that we feel when we are between old and new lives, or old and new relationships, roles, routines, and assumptions about ourselves.

Sometimes we only glimpse the neutrality of that time after we emerge from it. Such was the case with thirty-eight-year-old Paige, who had always expected to be married and have children. Since her marriage at age twenty-nine, however, she had had a series of miscarriages, followed by a long period of being unable to conceive. Finally, she was told by her doctor that she would never be able to bear a child. When asked how she had coped with her disappointment, Paige described a sad and solitary region, a space that only seemed wise to her in retrospect:

> To begin, I took time off from my job and then only went back to work on a part-time basis. I slept, read, grieved, and then sank into a fairly deep depression that lasted a year and a half. I gained weight and began to look terrible. But I can see that time for mourning is over. Right now, I am beginning to realize that there is life, even without bearing a child, though that is a hard pill for me to swallow. Still I know it's time to move on and, finally, I feel I'm ready.

Rather than consider this "lost" time as a foolish indulgence, Paige needed to regard that year and a half as a wise reprieve for herself. When uncertainty and sadness seem paralyzing, sometimes crawling under the covers is the most gentle and prudent course we can allow ourselves.

FINDING A PLACE TO CALL HOME

Sociologist Helen Rose Fuchs Ebaugh takes a slightly different look at this process of leaving old roles, or what she calls the "role exit process." In her wildly varied interviews with former doctors, dentists, police officers, air traffic controllers, teachers, military personnel, athletes, professors, convicts, prostitutes, transvestites, and nuns, she found that role exit is a unique process that demands our attention. "Role exit is a process of disengagement from a role that is central to one's self-identity and the reestablishment of an identity in a new role that takes into account one's ex-role."[5] For this reason, role exit must be a process that occurs over time. The same holds true for taking leave of old dreams. Imagine a woman who has doubts about leaving a role (that of doctor, nun, or teacher, for example) or giving up on a lost dream (bearing a child, becoming a company executive, and so forth). That person will begin to search for new roles and finally an alternative role—or dream—will be chosen. Still, the old and the new roles will jostle for position within her.

That is, each of our alternative roles or dreams will contain the residue of the previous roles. Of course, we know this to be true in many aspects of life, with countless illustrations in both literature and politics. When Eugene O'Neill's early plays rebelled against melodrama, for example, many aspects of those very plays were melodramatic. When dictators are toppled by popular uprisings, those revolutions often carry the seeds of dictatorship within them. So too our own new roles bear traces of our pasts.

Consider the lives of two teachers, for example, one of whom is a former member of a religious order, the other a former police officer. Both of these teachers will naturally approach their tasks as distinct individuals, but especially in the context of their previous roles. Similarly, when we let go of a dream, we still carry with us the shapes and hopes of that other era. This "hangover identity," as Ebaugh calls it, becomes a vital part of the next stage.

Just how vital was apparent in the case of Lydia, who bemoaned her apparent lack of a hangover identity. "At least my friends who are divorced or widowed have the status of having had a relationship. I have never been engaged or married. I am forty years old and have no status as someone who has even had a serious relationship." As Lydia refocuses on her dreams for the future, she will need to examine what was unique in her previous role, because in a sense each of us needs a hangover identity, just as each of us needs, has, and cannot escape a past. For some individuals, whose past roles in certain areas have seemingly been to "do without," the need to refocus on that past may be especially crucial.

As Lydia decided to embrace her single life with more exuberance, to quit waiting for "Mr. Right," as she put it, and to begin traveling more, she needed to carry an identity from the past that was meaningful. Lydia decided that she had two aspects of a past identity that were worth noting, that she would carry with her as she embarked on this new, more exciting "phase" of life. To begin with, she had been an active volunteer in a local hospital. This generosity had given her medical knowledge and an understanding of people under stress. In addition, Lydia had been a person afraid of risks. This bit of self-knowledge would not "hang over" in a negative sense, but would help her understand others who seem shy or aloof. Perhaps the role that Lydia was leaving was less defined than that of wife, fiancée, or parent, but these aspects of identity could—and did—prove enriching as she rethought her life and moved on. By refocusing, Lydia learned to avoid the trap of self-repudiation: "If only I hadn't been so shy. If only I had taken the initiative to make more friends. If only, if only. . . ." "If onlys" can only be categorized as "toxic waste" and serve no useful purpose in this journey. Our glance should be forward and our hope in the present.

NON-EVENT VARIETY: ONE LENS DOESN'T FIT ALL

Non-events come in at least four distinct varieties. Some are personal (your own non-event); some are ripple (losses you experience because of another's non-event); some are resultant (the consequence of an event that happens to you); and some are merely delayed (the events that eventually occur). Let's examine the directions that refocusing can take for each.

PERSONAL

These non-events might include not having a baby, not receiving a job promotion, or not following a desired career path. Essentially, though, such non-events primarily happen to you. You expect an event to occur and it doesn't. For example, if you've been locked into the same job for twenty years, your situation might be an example of nothing happening, yet everything changing for you inside. Further, if an expected job change doesn't occur, it might alter your assumptions about competence and identity.

Sam was a training director at a major corporation who reported being "thunderstruck" when he heard our description of non-events. "It's a compelling notion," he told us. "I'd like to steal your idea to help me explain a lot in my own life." It seems that from the time he was a child and well into his twenties, Sam's relationship with his father was virtually non-existent. His father never played ball with him, never went on walks, to sports events, or even on family vacations. Nor could Sam recall talking to his father, touching him, or, not surprisingly, feeling that his father cared about him.

Despite the obvious pain of this lifelong non-event, Sam was beginning to shift his focus. We found his reflection remarkable and an example of how rethinking can move us from regret to resolution. Sam told us at a subsequent interview:

> *I have come to realize that I no longer need to fight and struggle for my father's love in order to live and be a whole human being. This [realization] has influenced my relationships with all authority figures. I feel less compelled to please my boss by being Mr. Cooperative and Compliant. I feel relieved that I no longer have to beat my head against the hard rock wall that was this impenetrable person of my father. It seems to open the path toward other possibilities that I haven't considered. Like realizing and enjoying the discovery of who I am. I have worked hard for years in a therapeutic situation, always feeling I had to fight the battle with my father and win or reach some definitive, decisive outcome like in a boxing match. It only occurred to me recently that I could simply abandon the ring altogether and I'd be okay and probably better off.*

By "abandoning the ring," Sam ceased to picture himself as in constant combat. By stepping out of this intensely personal, metaphorical match, Sam began to move from inner conflict and toward new attitudes and relations.

RIPPLE

It should be obvious by now that non-events do not come in tidy packages. And they don't just happen to an individual. A non-event for one person may ripple into another's life. Thus a ripple non-event occurs when someone else's non-event triggers your own. For example, you don't become a grandparent because your children don't have children, you don't reconcile with a parent or child because that individual never seeks treatment for substance abuse. You don't pass on the family business because your son or daughter moves when a spouse relocates for work.

Ellen's relationship with her daughter Kay has been altered by what Ellen perceives as an enormous non-event. This past year, her thirty-two-year-old daughter told her mother she is a lesbian. Hoping to be closer to her mother after this admission and wanting to heal the resultant hurt, Kay is distraught that Ellen cannot accept her as she is. Ellen now wrestles with the fact that her daughter will never marry and will probably never give her grandchildren, and that she herself strongly disapproves of the daughter's lifestyle. "This has left me heartbroken," Ellen told us. "And it isn't even my own situation." Actually, in a way, it is. Kay's "non-event" is not marrying in the traditional sense, because this option is not legally possible or currently desirable for her. Fortunately, in the daughter's case, she has reshaped her dreams and entered into a committed partnership with another woman. But while Kay is at peace, Ellen still struggles for resolution.

In an age in which extended families are scattered and the nuclear family is stretched unbearably thin, our need for connection is stronger than ever before. It is for this reason that other people's non-events may ripple and affect us more deeply than in years past, when larger extended families met so many of our emotional needs. Curiously, the absence of a close relationship with another male (father, friend, or brother) surfaced several times during our surveys of men. Enrico reported a ripple non-event: that he had "always wanted to have someone in my life to call 'Dad.' But because my mother never had a permanent relationship with a man, I was raised by my mother, grandmother, and three older sisters. Not having a father was out of my control, could never be changed, and made me feel robbed. I had to really convince myself that you can be a whole person and not have a strong male influence on you. For me, this re-labeling process has been hard." What Enrico failed to realize, however, is that giving new names to our heartache is just the first step. Rethinking ourselves and our situations must follow if we are to leave disappointments behind. Nowhere is this more important than with failed personal relationships. In Enrico's case, his loss proceeded from his mother's loss. There was nothing he could do to change his mother's misfortune, but he could rethink his own reactions and chart new courses for male companionship. Letting go and reframing can become a wonderful release from old heartaches.

RESULTANT

Sometimes non-events occur because of events themselves. We have seen resultant non-events, for example, with parents who are forced to grapple with their children's disabilities. There can be some wonderful endings to these stories, but the birth of a severely handicapped child (the event) can signal the end to the dream of a healthy child (the non-event). Or a rejection from medical school can lead to the resultant non-event of not becoming a physician. Events in this sense can be seen as having a beginning and an end. Not having a healthy child or being a physician, on the other hand, can last a lifetime.

Career non-events also require a shifting of focus and often they are the result of events that are completely out of our control. Bob reported his bitter frustration when his company began to downsize considerably: "My disappointment was finally realizing that I was not having the 'perfect' career and was not establishing a straight-line path to career success. At first I felt removed from friends, since many of my friends in other companies were feeling good about making progress. It made me feel that my lack of progress was due to some deficit in me—even though the signs of company trouble had been apparent for some time." When asked where he was in his thinking at the time of the interview, Bob reported that he was "still formulating. I am continually rationalizing my thoughts and actions. I know I have to either redefine how I see my present job and how I define being stuck in the same place—or else I have to move on. Everyone else is moving ahead and I feel as if nothing is happening to me. I guess I should try to make something happen, though, because this company is hurting—and frankly, I am too."

As we study adult lives, it becomes clear that we need to honor discontinuity and not discount its value. This is especially true when the discontinuity is not of our own making. Like Bob, we can bemoan life's unfairness and long for circumstances to change. But sometimes the only course when reality is unyielding is simply to let go.

DELAYED

While most adults keenly felt the loss of their dreams, many perceived their losses as delayed events and felt that there was still time for marriage, a career move, or even the conception of a child. Unfortunately, as time passes, these losses increasingly transform into non-events. When this transition happens, some adults begin to give up hope and lose confidence in their ability to shape the future.

Connor, for example, was sure he'd never be promoted. As an administrative assistant in a printing company for nine years, he had neither education nor training to move to the desktop department nor seniority to become an executive assistant. But as the secretarial pool grew, Connor saw a need for better coordination. Six months after approaching his boss, he became the office manager. Of course, not only was his promotion merely a delayed event, but Connor had turned the situation around himself by rethinking his current status and reframing how he saw himself in the workplace.

So how can these non-event distinctions help us better

shape our thinking? When we clarify the source of our non-events, our refocusing is sharper and new goals loom more readily into view.

REFOCUSING, REFRAMING, AND OTHER OPTIC STRATEGIES

Leaving our old roles and seeing our way toward new ones can be a painful process in surprisingly uncharted territory. The will to see is not just the province of new and high technology. In ancient times, Buddha reminded his followers that on the path to noble enlightenment, "right view" precedes "right thinking." The Psalmist asked God to enlighten his eyes that he might return to joy (Ps. 13:3), and Jesus, years later, instructed that the "lamp of the body is the eye. It follows that if your eye is sound, your whole body will be filled with light" (Matt. 6:22). The teachings of these masters speak to the universality of certain truths. To return to our modern metaphors: We have to be willing to regard our personal dilemmas with a fresh gaze. But that can only occur if we are willing to relinquish our old ways of seeing.

LETTING GO OF EXPECTATIONS

Though letting go is essential to new vision, this is easier said than done. When we relinquish a dream, we first need to remove some internal blinders, then change our self-assumptions. Without those first steps, letting go is almost unthinkable. Still, according to many psychologists, this surrender is crucial to development. As children, for example, we believe that our parents are omnipotent and that life is simple and somehow manageable. However, as we grow older, these early assumptions are inevitably challenged. For time is not endless; we can never have it all, and often we need to rethink our very selves when family scripts have pigeonholed us unfairly.

Of course, some assumptions are essential for our very existence. At any age, we hold on to beliefs about ourselves, our world, and our relationships because we need some guarantees just to get out of bed in the morning! When a non-event destroys that delicate balance, however, we need to let go of assumptions that no longer serve their purpose.

We think of the story of the little girl who used to swing out over a pond, using a rope tied to a large tree. At first the child was frightened and could not make herself abandon the rope and fall into the water. But each time she refused to risk the plunge, the child would crash back into the tree. Finally, scratched and bleeding from the experience, she took a deep breath, swung out as far as possible—and let go.

Unfortunately, we see scratched and bleeding children around us all the time. Maureen confided that she had called her therapist feeling frantic. Her unmarried daughter, who still did not have steady work or career plans, had not called her mother for several days. Maureen was concerned that her daughter's non-events—no marriage and no career—were permanent. She was also concerned that her daughter would forget a promising job interview. When the therapist asked, "How old is your daughter?" (she already knew the answer), Maureen's embarrassed response of "twenty-eight" said it all. Both mother and daughter needed to let go of their unproductive involvement in each other's lives. In this particular relationship, the daughter shared her agonies about employment and relationships with her mother, and her mother in turn would respond with protectiveness and anger. This led Maureen to conduct a job search for her daughter, and the emotional involvement went from bad to worse. Obviously, trying to orchestrate another person's life (or alleviate another's non-event) can be futile, if not downright destructive.

In *Necessary Losses*,[6] Judith Viorst writes of this need to let go of our dreams for our children—expectations often held unconsciously before these sons and daughters were even born.

And yet, letting these expectations go will free the next generation to shape their own lives. The same holds true for expectations about our parents, spouses, siblings, and friends. When we
let go of all those metaphorical ropes, we learn to accept others
as they are.

Sometimes the connections are so imperfect, however,
especially in our work lives, that a complete and clean separation
becomes essential. This was certainly true for Bob, whose company was struggling to survive, and who needed to let go of his
unavailing expectations. Eventually, he saw the futility of his situation, and let go of his dead-end job to seek employment at
another company. The move involved a cut in salary, but Bob
reports that this new company is healthier and holds promise for
advancement. In the end, letting go meant relief in the present
and a more satisfying career down the line.

FACING YOUR ILLUSIONS:
A DOUBLE-EDGED SWORD

In her research on the role of illusions in various aspects
of living, social psychologist Shelley E. Taylor, author of *Positive
Illusions*, studied women with breast cancer. Curiously, she found
that those women who believed, against the odds, in their recovery did better than those facing all the negative possibilities. As a
consequence, Taylor found that "normal human thought and
perception is marked not by accuracy but by positive self-
enhancing illusions about the self, the world, and the future."[7]
Furthermore, such "illusions" may actually be indicative of good
mental health. In fact, far from detracting from the healing
process, these illusions of recovery provided a protective device
that seemed to promote that very prospect.

The body-mind connection has been well explored in
recent years, but Taylor makes a particularly intriguing point
when she notes that a good perception can be more helpful than
a raw reality.

That being said, there is also a downside to illusions. Irvin Yalom, author of *Love's Executioner*, presents the contrasting view when he maintains that "though illusion often cheers and comforts, it ultimately and invariably weakens and constricts the spirit."[8] Yalom, a psychotherapist, describes several cases in which his strategy was to force the patient to face illusions. In one case, Yalom confronted the client by pushing her to the realization that some of her grief over her father's lonely life was really misplaced. It was her own life, not her father's, that was tragically unfulfilled.

Could Taylor and Yalom both be correct? We believe they are, but that it depends upon the situation. In areas of personal health and healing, Taylor's research is well founded. But in other areas of life, where reality is less subjective, theories like those of Yalom have much to teach us. Consider the case of Elena, a woman in her late sixties, who faced the most challenging non-event of her career. Elena's event had been devastating—being fired from a job she loved, for reasons she could not understand. At the time of her firing, Elena reported feeling grief-stricken, but immediately she began the search for another job, all the while networking with former colleagues and talking to several head hunters. But Elena's major event soon induced an even more significant non-event. Increasingly she realized that her letters of application were not being answered nor her phone calls returned. Over the next weeks, Elena began to attribute this silence to age bias, and she soon felt helpless in the face of a situation beyond her control. In addition, Elena had worked all her life and expected to work until she "dropped," as she stoically put it. Being fired was an indisputable shock, but realizing that she might never be employed again seemed even more catastrophic.

As Elena confided:

I felt bruised, hostile, and miserable. I fantasized that those who fired me would come crawling back begging me to go back to my job. I hoped I would tell them to go to hell. I went through a rough period for a while, but as I reassessed my situation, I discovered that I never wanted to look for a job again. Nor will I work from nine to five in an office. Because I knew that age hadn't diminished my ability or robbed me of my experience, I began to see myself as having some options. Now I am a consultant working out of my house. True, I have no colleagues, but neither do I have any bosses or people to supervise. I have adopted a new dream—being on my own, working at home.

However comforting the illusion that experience and competence will usually win out, Elena needed to face the reality that, however unfair the practice might be, most companies would not hire an adult of her age. At first, that knowledge was frightening, but ultimately it gave her the freedom to make new choices. So when is facing reality better than holding illusions? We suggest it's primarily when that reality is truly—and completely—out of our control.

REFRAMING THE PICTURE

"Reframing" occurs when we redefine our non-events or our ability to cope with them—a strategy similar to restoring an old family picture that's grown badly faded.

In this manner, a situation can be perceived as comic, tragic, or somewhere in between. It can also be viewed as a curse or a gift, an irritation or a relief. Here's how one woman took a blow to her career and reframed the experience dramatically.

From her earliest college years, Maile had dreamed of becoming a partner in a large law firm. But this was no idle dream. She prepared by attending a good law school, making law review, clerking for a well-known judge, and finally joining a major law firm near her hometown. Three years after she began at the firm, however, Maile married and within two more years was the mother of twins. At that point, she decided to cut back to forty hours a week instead of the expected sixty. In adjusting her schedule, Maile hoped that because she was creative and hardworking she would be rewarded. But each year, when the new partners were voted in, Maile was passed over. Finally she realized she would never make partner as long as she wanted a balanced life. At first, Maile was depressed that she had spent so many years preparing for a goal that would never be realized. At this stage, she was stuck in thinking of her career in a linear fashion and in defining herself primarily as a respected law partner.

Then Maile began talking to other working mothers and reading books on women's issues. These discussions of the narrow scripts that women follow—scripts too confining for their actual roles at work, in the family, and in society at large—began to jar her thinking. Slowly Maile questioned some long-held views about herself, and in doing so, she was surprised to find her lack of promotion presented even better possibilities. Why did she need to be a partner in a large law firm? There were many ways to live her life as a woman, a lawyer, a mother, and wife. For Maile, not making partner forced her to reframe her own views of success.

Ironically, some of the very attributes that make Maile a fine lawyer were useful in changing these views. Psychologist Martin Seligman contends that optimism is a key determinant in a healthy life, and he provides strategies for becoming more optimistic. One of these techniques he calls "disputation," a process of self-arguing or disputing our negative beliefs by showing that they are incorrect. Instead of fearing that she was not top "legal material," Maile disputed that negative interpretation and reframed it to say: "I choose to be enriched in several areas in my life. And, further, I am unwilling to pay the price for excelling in only one." Similarly, a woman who faces infertility can reframe her own situation by using another new script. Instead of anguishing endlessly because "I am someone who cannot conceive," she can first dispute that negative actuality and then recast it to say with conviction, "I am someone who wants to parent a child and I can do this through adoption."

As Seligman notes, "Ducking our disturbing beliefs can be a good first aid, but a deeper, more lasting remedy is to dispute them: Give them an argument. Go on the attack. By effectively disputing the beliefs that follow adversity, you can change your customary reaction from dejection."[9]

Elena disputed the harsh reality of age bias and rethought her place in the workforce. For their part, Maile and Bob were unwilling to submit to crushing workloads or a company's poor treatment of its workers. But before these three individuals could make the next move, they needed to let go of their old dreams and reframe some new realities. Over the course of many months they were able to do just that.

RITES OF PASSAGE: OUTWARD SIGNS OF INNER CHANGE

When we reflect on rites of passage, we tend to think of tribal customs or ancient rituals that marked a young person's passage to adulthood. That is probably because we are a nation where such rites are less obvious. Other than the Jewish traditions of Bar and Bat Mitzvah, the Native American vision quest, and the Amish and Mennonite designated dress codes, few religious and social groups have outward rites that delineate the passage from childhood to adulthood so clearly. Rather, our coming-of-age rituals are more subtle, more secular—a fact that dates back many years. In our grandparents' day, the rites of bobbing hair and wearing long trousers signaled a certain maturity and status. And in our own time, attaining a driver's license seems to indicate that an important threshold has been crossed.

But passage rites signify more than just a progression to adulthood. They are intended to outwardly announce a significant inner change. In any rite of passage, the person is separated from the familiar. Then ensues the uncomfortable time of leaving a former life (or dream) behind—an important interval in which rites can ease the transition to the next state, when finally the person is incorporated into a new role.

Sometimes, though, we simply need rituals of continuity, not passage. Unlike the latter, which connote movement, continuity rituals are important for the stability they provide. We know the larger rituals of culture in this country that bind our years and our seasons. From Thanksgiving to Christmas, at least our stores and commercial worlds insist upon that knowledge. But, Hallmark and merchants aside, we need these ritual reminders of physical and spiritual stability. For this reason, we require rituals within our families and circles of friends—holiday traditions, blessings before dinner, shared meals, the spinning of old yarns and the storing of memories, bedtime stories, and evening walks. But whatever customs we use to cloak ourselves, we well know the comfort and importance of such rituals.

Unfortunately, non-events are too often bereft of either rites of passage or ritual. But without these outward signs to remind us of our progress and our place, how can we expect ourselves to feel located in new roles? Our rites of passage and rituals are symbols of something larger. Much like flags and wedding bands, these symbols stand publicly for a deeper truth. We have only to consider the emotional outcry about flag burning in this country or to regard our newly engaged friends (with their suddenly conspicuous hands) to know that symbols can be vital to our sense of emerging selves.

This is why we believe that non-events deserve their own kind of observances. These may be intensely personal rites that serve as outward signs that something within has changed. Or they may be comforting rituals, each somehow a reminder that the essence of us remains. The point is that both rites and rituals have their rightful place in refocusing. As we move, we remember who we were, who we are, and who we have yet to become.

Charlotte and her coauthor finally got their play produced. True, it was in a small community theater, but it was performed. Several of their friends expressed admiration that they could persist in peddling it to producers for ten years, wondering how they dealt with so much rejection. With each rejection, however, the two playwrights and their husbands bought a bottle of champagne and toasted the play. As Charlotte said, "We remember the ten years not as a struggle but as a series of celebrations."

We also were delighted to find humor lurking in other non-events. An article in *Ms.* magazine, for example, addressed the issue of being single and reproduced the following announcement that a woman had sent to friends to celebrate her single state.[10] It read:

> *Alice and Carl Hesse*
> *are pleased to announce their daughter*
> *Susan A. Hesse*
> *is settling into*
> *Joyous Old Maidhood*
> *after which she shall cease*
> *looking for Mr. Right*
> *and begin giving*
> *scintillating dinner parties and soirees.*
> *To help celebrate this wonderful occasion*
> *gift-place-settings*
> *are available at*
> *Macy's Department Store*

While these authors might deplore the label "Old Maidhood," the message is clear—this woman had selected her own rite of passage and was clearly about to get on with her life!

How else can we observe our non-events? Observance might mean burying a symbolic object in the backyard to signify an ending. Or taking yourself to an elegant restaurant to celebrate the beginning of personal freedom after a job or relationship has ended. We remember Delia, a woman near seventy who decided to abandon her dream of remarriage. Not that it wasn't possible, but her anxious life-on-hold had persisted long enough. Delia's rite of freedom entailed hiring a personal trainer and getting her body in shape for herself. "This is my way of saying, 'I may not be looking to marry again, but I'm not too old to be attractive.'"

We were also rather taken with the creativity of another young woman, whose self-declared non-event was the absence of an appropriate mate. Melinda had undertaken many projects but they had "never seemed complete or satisfying without a companion." In particular, she had bought a fifty-year-old house in serious need of renovation, but despite her personal aptitude for repairs, Melinda felt that this was a project that demanded a close, male counterpart. Then on her fortieth birthday, she decided to reframe her thinking. Melinda's rite of passage? "I went into the bathroom that morning with a crowbar and started swinging. I could do it! Destroy the old and build up the new! Just me! By myself! I can't describe how free I felt that day."

Your own rites of passage may be less dramatic, but the point is to create some satisfying sign that you're about to move on. For rites and rituals, in the end, are merely strategies to help you shift the focus from what you have longed for to what can truly be yours.

9

Reshaping the Dream

This is the moment of embarking.

All auspicious signs are in place.

—DENG MING-DAO[1]

Here's a thought that strikes a discordant note in many of us: New Year's resolutions. But why should the very mention of these promises make us feel uncomfortable? Generally it's because our New Year's resolutions reflect what we haven't done or become in the previous year: thinner, calmer, more productive, more self-controlled, and so on. In essence, whatever our resolutions, they seem to imply who we are not. The flip side, of course, is that resolutions can be hardy, healthy beginnings at the start of a new day or time or year. From the Latin word to loosen or unbind, resolutions to change have been formalized in the world's great religions—for example, in Yom Kippur, the Jewish Day of Atonement; in Ramadan, the Islamic month of fasting; or in the Catholic Sacrament of Reconciliation, more frequently called Confession.

Whether formal or not, resolutions entail choices. In this last step of the dream-reshaping process, we see the individual facing choices for the future—choices that lead to multiple paths or a continuum of options.

How much choice do we really have? Is our decision to hold on to a dream, to modify it, or to let it go completely in our control? Neither totally free nor rigidly determined, most of us find that many factors influence us by degrees. Each of us, for example, is shaped to some extent by sex, a genetic pool, family dynamics, social class, cultures, and subcultures. Further, we can't choose our body type, our country of origin, our place in the sibling birth order, or the finances of our family. And later in life, we seem to have fewer options in an overwhelming world: We can't prevent earthquakes or floods, force a company to keep us on the payroll, or oblige another person to fall irrevocably in love. So where do we have choices?

To begin with, even in the worst of circumstances, we can choose how to react in a given situation. We can also choose how to act in the future, deciding where to invest both our energies and our hearts.

POSSIBLE DREAM PATHS

A dream path really suggests a continuum of paths: holding on to a dream, modifying the dream, or reshaping it altogether. Before you assess how to pursue these choices, however, let's examine what they imply with a few examples.

Imagine you are looking for a job, longing for a baby, or searching for a meaningful relationship. If you believe that each of these dreams is only delayed, you might well hold on to your particular dream, believing time and fortune are on your side. On the other hand, if you've tried unsuccessfully to realize that dream and (in your mind, at least) you've waited long enough, you may decide it's time to modify your expectations.

For example, you finally realize you'll never play professional baseball, despite your considerable talent. In time, you may decide to become a high-school or college coach. Or you reshape that particular dream altogether and become a stockbroker or real-estate agent with a continuing interest in professional sports. In each case, your decision about a possible dream path will be based on assessing your *self*, *supports*, *situation*, and *strategies*. It will also be grounded in the essential element of hope.

REVISITING HOPE

Throughout this book, we have examined heartbreak, hope, and healing. The heartbreak aspect is clear. Hope, as we've seen, is more complex.

If there's still hope that your non-event will change into an event, you might hold on to your dream and plan new ways to realize it. But if your situation is clearly hopeless, perhaps you'll choose to reshape your dream. The complication, as you may have surmised from your own situation, arises when hope is ambiguous, when possibility isn't probability yet and the future seems in limbo.

Sometimes we hold on to hope unrealistically by filtering reality in such a way that we ignore the signals that this dream will never be realized. Like many of us, Andrea filtered her reality for quite a while. At forty-two, she had been divorced for years and raised her two children to adulthood. For a long time after the divorce, Andrea had been very involved with Keith, a younger but supportive schoolteacher with whom she had planned a committed future. After nearly seven years of being together, however, Andrea began to see the evidence that had been there all along. While very affectionate and generally understanding of her situation as a single mother, Keith had never connected to Andrea's children, had rarely shared the extra expenses from his frequent stays at her house, and had not once mentioned marriage and settling down. Finally, Andrea delivered an ultimatum: We get married within the next year or this relationship is over. Shocked, hurt, but not ready to commit, Keith ended the affair. "I gave some of the best years of my adulthood to that relationship," Andrea told us, "and I kept hoping that he wanted something deeper. Ultimately, we just wanted very different things and neither could deliver what the other needed."

Sometimes our hope centers on dreams for our careers. At thirty-six, Matt too had experienced false starts and disappointments before transforming his dream of owning a car dealership. For a long time, Matt had held to the belief that his work as a car mechanic and his wife's as a bookkeeper would enable them to save enough to achieve their goal. But after five years, with his consistently modest salary, Matt realized the impossibility of even saving for a down payment. At that point, he gave up this particular dream and began to transform himself and his goals. He still wanted to run his own business, but he tailored that dream to reality and became an independent mechanic, working out of space that he was able to rent. As Matt acknowledged:

> *I began to accept the reality that I would always be a blue-collar worker, but I could be happy with myself as an honest, hardworking person. At first I felt I had failed, but now I know better. I'm working harder being my own boss, but the satisfaction is greater. So's the money.*

Like Andrea and Matt, each of us must answer certain questions as we assess our choices. Some of them might be: Is it time to give up the dream? Am I deluding myself in thinking my goal is possible for me? Or am I giving up too quickly?

There are no true formulas upon which to base your answers, but the 75 percent rule has been useful to some. It goes like this: If 75 percent of the time you are unhappy, confused, anxious, or otherwise miserable about a situation and these feelings have persisted for some time, the chances are good that it's time to relinquish the dream.

Observing the experience of others can also be instructive, as we see first with Marian, whose dream was transformed consciously, and then with Daniel, whose dreams changed gradually as new circumstances evolved.

THE SLOW ROAD HOME

Marion, it seemed, was living a life of non-events, not realizing that they caused her feelings of hopelessness.

> *My marriage did not work out—a really shattered dream. My son and his wife and child moved in with me, clearly an event. But*

it stemmed from a non-event—my son not being like other people's sons and having skills and motivation to be self-supporting. My professional life also became a non-event. I had wanted to become an accountant. That was derailed because there never seemed to be time or money to prepare for the CPA exam. Although I became an office manager, that did not carry the prestige or salary that being an accountant does. Still, I thought it was a ticket up the ladder. Then followed a series of circumstances that led to my being fired.

At this point, Marion sought relief from her feelings of despair.

I went into therapy. My life was falling apart. Nothing was going as planned. Eventually, through living and therapy, I decided to make things happen. I have been trying desperately since then to reshape my original dreams of work and family. Fortunately, therapy has helped me enormously. Though I still feel great loss, I'm less angry and depressed. Getting up in the morning and facing the day is much easier, and that's a big step for me.

In addition to contending with feelings of loss, Marian decided to reshape both her thinking and her life. To begin with, she had accepted the relatively new cultural myth that women must excel at everything. After all the shame, guilt, and depression that followed being fired, Marian understood that reshaping her dream first would require freeing herself (again the "loosening" or "unbinding" of resolutions). This time the freedom would be from myths she had internalized about careers, success, parenting, and women in general. Though Marian's internal journey, like all of ours, was neither linear nor easy, the following suggests the possible paths that she considered and ultimately chose.

At first, Marian *held on to her dreams* and accepted the definitions of success that pervade much of modern thinking. These included her perceived "total responsibility" for the outcome of her son's life, as well as the mandate to excel as a career woman.

Then Marian became a woman disappointed in herself, her son, and her career, but hoping to get back on track with each aspect of her life. In time, however, she relinquished these myths for both herself and for her child. And eventually this "unbinding" was part of her resolution to *modify one dream* and completely *reshape another*. Ultimately, Marian entered a helping field, working with displaced homemakers. At the same time, she has let go of her son's mental illness as her fault and responsibility. Is Marian content now or more at peace? Today she reports:

> *I have found myself again. Only this time it's a better, freer self. All the external changes in my life—a new career, new friends, a more realistic relationship with my son—each of these is a reflection of some internal changes I've made. That's the secret, or at least it was for me. I needed to completely rethink myself and as I did, my old despair seemed to lift.*

A THOUSAND POSSIBLE LIVES

We see a somewhat different scenario in Daniel's life, one that unfolded in ways he never would have predicted. If he has any regrets, he told us, it is that he let go of his dream too soon. His life, in fact, is an example of the way many people live their lives—without making informed choices. In Daniel's case, he didn't make a conscious decision to give up becoming a musician: Circumstances just seemed to overtake him.

As a child, Daniel constantly played the piano, wrote show tunes, and worked in different bands. Then World War II broke out and Daniel was shipped overseas. After the war, he and his wife moved to a tiny apartment in New York City—so small there was no room for a piano. Still committed to music,

Daniel arranged to place his piano with a friend and enrolled in a music school on the G.I. Bill. At this point, his dream of a career in music seemed in motion.

But once again, external events—this time personal—interfered. His wife became pregnant and Daniel felt tremendous pressure to start making money. Dropping out of music school, he took a temporary job in retailing. It turned into his lifetime career.

We know, of course, that there are no "right ways" to live a life, that each of us indeed has a thousand possible lives. As Daniel acknowledges:

> I may be "wistful," but I'm not in despair about my life choices. Each of us could have gone down one of several paths—I believe that's the whole point of Frost's poem "The Road Not Taken." Personally, a part of me will always long for the stage, but I wouldn't trade my wife and children and even the physical comfort I now enjoy, for anything. It's actually good to be able to say that because it makes the truth of those words more real for me.

SEEDS OF TRANSFORMATION

Whether you let go of your dream entirely, like Daniel, or hold on longer and then modify your dream, like Marian, your success with a new goal will depend on the resources and strengths that you bring to this transition. Here we take a look at assessing these assets or taking stock.

Psychologist Bernice Neugarten reminds us that adults are continually stocktaking or monitoring themselves. During this silent assessment, questions like the following emerge (however unconsciously): How am I doing? Am I where I want to be with regard to my self? My family? My work? My loved ones? The answers to these questions may yield a sense of being "on time" or "off-time." But people may also make a self-assessment or take stock to see if they have the resources for changing their lives.[2]

One means of taking stock as we consider reshaping our dreams is to ask and answer the following questions: Do we have good *strategies* for achieving our dreams? Do we have a vision of our *self* that impels us to change? Do we have the *supports* to help us? Are our *situations* such that we can consider transformation?

This self-assessment system is predicated upon a number of assumptions:

- ❦ There is no one factor that is essential for coping with change. Your own resources are many and their combinations highly individual.
- ❦ Everyone has a balance of both resources and deficits as they face life transitions.
- ❦ There are steps you can take to change the deficits into resources.[3]

If your resources are strong, of course, you're in a better position to take a risk or make a change. If they aren't, however, you may wish to defer more major changes until they are. Either way, by taking stock of your *strategies, self, supports,* and *situation,* you can assess how well equipped you are to deal with any transition. And by assessing these resources, you can identify your strengths and note which ones need bolstering.

YOUR STRATEGIES: CONSCIOUS COPING

As you proceed with your own dream reshaping, you'll need to assess which coping strategies to use. Rather than chronicle a list of possible strategies, we suggest that two categories described by psychologists Richard Lazarus and Susan Folkman provide a means to organize your thinking about the future. In their research, Lazarus and Folkman found that most coping strategies fall into one of two categories—*problem-focused*, which center on changing the source of the stress, and *emotion-focused*, which help people manage their feelings and change their thinking.[4]

When hope abounds: Using problem-focused strategies.

There are many instances when an "old" dream might still be realized. In those cases, *problem-focused* coping strategies are the most appropriate. According to Lazarus and Folkman, problem-focused strategies can be used to take control and thereby remove the barrier that turned an expectation into a non-event. One standard way of taking control is through problem solving or brainstorming. Joan's major non-event was not getting a permanent teaching position at the college level after her first three-year contract. To make matters worse, the reason she was denied the position had no relevance to Joan's qualifications or track record. Her teaching department simply had one too many professors and the old saw "Last to come; first to go" prevailed in Joan's case.

> *I had identified with the academic world as a Ph.D. professor. Now I no longer belonged to that world. I perceived anything else as a loss of status. I lost control of my schedule, but of even more importance, I lost confidence. I felt my aspirations were all wasted.*

Eventually Joan took control by deliberate problem solving and brainstorming through a course on career and life planning. "Taking the course was a stretch. I learned how to plan my career and now it doesn't scare me," she explained. Joan also found she was able to accomplish two important changes:

1. She calmed her fears and strengthened her self-confidence.
2. She took stock of her talents and preferences so she could better plan her future.

Today Joan has her own consulting business, in which she writes grant proposals for companies in her field. This career provides a fairly steady income while allowing her the satisfaction of interacting with clients. In a sense, she's still teaching. Only the audiences have changed.

When Tina's oldest son was diagnosed as severely learning disabled and no local school could adequately meet his needs, Tina started her own school. In this new environment, with teachers who accommodated the learning styles of her son and other children, she helped her family and changed her own career. Today that child is a productive, well-educated member of society. And Tina? She and her school are thriving.

Though from the beginning Tina refused to take "no" when it came to educating her child, other respondents had to learn to say "no" in order to control their own lives. Candace, thirty-eight, had been in a deteriorating marriage for ten years with an abusive alcoholic. After exploring many solutions— therapy, pleading, modified behavior, temporary separations— she realized that her dream of a loving marriage with this man was futile. Finally, Candace asserted herself and left a destructive non-event. Today she is happily remarried and wiser for the experience. "If only I had said 'no' earlier," Candace told us.

But we caution against "if onlys." Candace did the best she could with the resources she had at the time. Too much of our lives can be wasted on regrets when we should be reshaping our dreams in the here and now.

When hope is absent: Using emotion-focused strategies.
What if our circumstances are impossible to change? If a situation seems hopeless, employing emotion-focused coping strategies can lessen the pain by distancing us from the source of the problem and helping us to reappraise and refocus. In other words, though we can't change the situation, we can change the way we evaluate it. Daniel clearly was not going to change his life, but he was reframing his life without music. And while he

might grieve for a lost career, he could well rejoice in the life he actually lives.

Of course, we often use both problem-focused and emotion-focused strategies simultaneously. But in general, when there is hope, action or problem-focused strategies can change the situation, and when there's not, emotion-focused ones can help us manage our reactions.

YOUR SELF:
DREAMING THE NEW AND THE POSSIBLE

Gloria Steinem, author and an early leader of the feminist movement, wrote about how she began to picture herself as a new, more hopeful woman—including how she would look, how she would walk, even what she would wear in the future. We too can picture a future self by allowing our subconscious to creep into consciousness, and by looking back and then forward with hope. As Steinem writes:

> Many therapists, shamans, and other wise women and men recommend checking in with that future self often, perhaps each morning as part of a daily meditation. [By] adding the inner child to that routine . . . there is contact with both the creativity that our child-self represents and the strength and wisdom of our future self.[5]

The way we see ourselves in the present is also critical in determining what we do about our unrealized dreams. For example, Steve had written two novels, neither of which had been published. His mother, on the other hand, had written seven novels, the first of which made The New York Times bestseller list. Following her first book, his mother was elated and fully expected to repeat this success. Her subsequent books were never even reviewed, however. Because her vision of herself was tied to public success, she died feeling a failure. Steve, on the other hand, gave up this dream early on. Since he enjoyed his career as a research director, writing bestsellers wasn't essential to his dream of self.

The difference between mother and son underscores an essential point: The meaning of a non-event and the resultant sense of self can only be determined by the person experiencing it. Steve assessed himself and found that he needed to change dreams—a shift he made with comparative ease because he'd invested less time and energy than his mother. And this is yet another advantage to self-assessment and honesty: If our personal talents or opportunities are wanting, it's futile to batter doors that are permanently closed. It also wastes valuable time.

YOUR SUPPORTS:
ALLIES AND ASSETS ALONG THE WAY

Most of us need the support of others, especially if we are transforming our possible paths or possible selves. Support can cover a range of activities, including affection from others (whether an expression of love or one of respect), affirmation (when others agree that your actions are appropriate or understandable), assistance or aid (help with tutoring, editing, caretaking, driving, or whatever support is needed), and feedback (responses that help you reinterpret situations, often providing a different perspective).

Russell was enthusiastic in his description of the friends who had helped him through a difficult divorce—with dinners out, ball games, movies, and even a couple of blind dates. "Though I'm now happily remarried and a father of two, I'll never forget the folks who loved and supported me during that rough spell. While I was busy beating myself up for a failed marriage, these buddies and their wives believed in me—and eventually I began to again as well."

YOUR SITUATION:
GRIM, GREAT, OR SOMEWHERE IN BETWEEN

A group of individuals all with what seems to be the same non-event—for example, no job—will obviously be in diverse situations and experience them differently. Some will have enormous stresses, and others few; some will have considerable financial resources, and others little; some will perceive that they have many options while others will envision virtually none. Your situation then will greatly influence whether you can consider a transformation. You will want to examine that situation closely to assess both its severity and some possible solutions. As we'll see, Jim did just that.

Phoenix rising: A survivor's story.
Jim's story is proof that human courage and resourcefulness can exist in the face of adversity. No life is problem-free, but this middle-aged man seemed to have suffered one major setback after another. And while his coping was neither methodical nor easy, Jim's life has steadily improved now thanks to some conscious reflection and subsequent choices.

Jim's situation. At fifty-five, Jim works in a social service agency for a program that is only funded from year to year. As a consequence, he has no retirement benefits and is forced to live modestly in an old house in the inner city. Also living with him is his adult son, an alcoholic who had been in and out of psychiatric institutions as a child and who now is unable to keep a job and unwilling to enter a rehabilitation program.

From Jim's point of view, each part of his life may be said to contain a non-event, the dream that went unrealized as time went by. First Jim's lost dream of family:

> *When we adopted Ben, he was eleven months old. He had been abandoned. We fell in love with him and felt that with a good environment he could make up for his early loss of trust. However,*

our lives fell apart when my wife, Jane, had a nervous breakdown. At first I tried to be supportive, but it was too much for me. Eventually we divorced and I gained custody of Ben. I worked hard at being a good father and felt terrible that Jane would have nothing to do with Ben. Then, over time, Ben became more and more difficult to handle.

I always expected that he would have "upper-middle-class values." Instead, he became so difficult that we had to put him in a state school, which he left before graduating. I know he will never be a high-school graduate, but I pray that he will stay out of jail now [he has already been in jail several times].

Then Jim's lost dream of career:

In terms of my career, I started on a master's degree in sociology, then decided to become an artist. I found working alone more satisfying than having to adjust to a bureaucracy. I worked hard, became fairly successful, as judged by the fact that my work was accepted in a number of juried shows. However, I only earned about fifteen thousand dollars a year from art. To supplement my income, I worked at a continuing education center teaching art. Then, at a certain point, I began volunteering at a rehabilitation center. I wrote several proposals that got funded and for the past five years have worked full-time for that organization in a "soft-money," no-benefits job. I love the work, but not the pay.

After examining his situation more carefully, Jim took further stock.

Jim's self: Jim's sense of self is strong.

I was very depressed as a young person, and over the years fought depression off and on. After many years of therapy I finally feel good about myself, if not about every aspect of my life. I have tal-

ent, courage, a sense of humor, and best of all, I have a sense of purpose. I honestly like who I am and what I'm trying to achieve.

Jim's supports: In this area, Jim's resources were weaker. To begin with, Jim told us that he regretted his lack of money. He loves his current job but worries about the future. Since his job depends on soft money, Jim wonders how he will support himself if the funds dry up. Currently, he has about ten thousand dollars in assets and a run-down house. Fortunately, by examining his financial support more carefully, Jim realized he needed to take action. Today, he's working with good friends to renovate his house and rent several rooms to students. Further, Jim promises, he plans to put this additional income into a retirement fund so that his future will grow more secure.

Jim has also surrounded himself with a rich network of friends. He belongs to Parents Without Partners, a group he attends sporadically now as he hosts more plaster-and-paint parties at his fast-improving home.

Jim's strategies: Jim has employed many strategies through the years. First, he used therapy and the support of good friends to change his attitude toward his problems. For Jim, this emotion-focused strategy changed his self-perception, the first key step to reshaping his lost dreams.

Through taking stock of his situation and various systems of support, Jim was able to gain better control of his future. Though his life is admittedly challenging, Jim has examined his non-events carefully and bolstered himself in each situation with emotional support from others and a strengthened sense of self. He's also made a conscious decision about each of his lost dreams.

In the area of having a partner, Jim has let this dream go. Though he doesn't rule out that possibility, he says he isn't actively seeking a mate nor does he now feel the need. Regarding his career, Jim has retained his love of art but modified that dream to include a slightly more lucrative job. While even this career is uncertain, Jim admits, the pay is better than what he made as an artist. And just as important to his present peace of mind is his plan to rent rooms. It will provide him with company in a rambling old house and bring in much-needed income.

Finally, in the area of family, Jim has reshaped that dream so that family includes his closest friends and the people he helps through his work. As for his son, he will always love him, but he's let go of all his old paternal expectations and established new boundaries in their relationship. The situation with Ben isn't ideal, but Jim has accepted what he can't change and changed what he can.

In summary, our dream paths are as varied as our individual lives—and within each life the choices are many. As we've seen, Jim's story illustrates that any non-event may have a variety of solutions and even those may differ as our resources and circumstances allow.

The important message for each of us is that paths and "reshaping" imply movement. Hope does too. For we'll never be stuck with a lost dream or a future devoid of promise as long as we're resolving and choosing and moving toward a goal. Perhaps that's the gift of New Year's after all—a starting gate with its annual call of "Mark, set . . . *go*."

Afterword:

From Heartache

to Hope

wo final words about lost dreams. Sometimes with a minimum of effort and just plain good fortune, the stories of our secret losses have surprise endings. Hillary, for example, the author of a new publication, is getting a great deal of attention. She told us that if her fiancé hadn't "jilted" her, she never would have moved to Washington, D.C., joined a policy organization, and written her book. Though Hillary's story is only one of many, we're not suggesting that every secret loss begets a happy surprise ending. But we do believe in being open to possibilities, knowing that many surprises await us, and that many of them are wonderful.

More typically, however, nothing is happening in our lives where something should be and this absence deserves our full attention. As we've seen, these lost dreams may include fruitless searches for the "right" mate, love fading or going sour, wondering "what might have been" if we'd married someone else, the sorrow of infertility, and disappointments with our children's lives. Similarly, when nothing happens in our careers, we can feel embarrassed, ashamed, and sad that what we expected never took place. In our secret legacy losses, we feel pain if we're unable to leave behind memories or evidence that we have "mattered" to others. And, of course, our most private losses, the ones connected to our dreams of self, can also change how we view ourselves and the world in sometimes shattering ways.

But these very losses provide our challenge: to search for the essence of our dreams, realizing that there are many possible paths and that this knowledge of options and alternatives can suggest new horizons, energy, and hope. For despite our lost dreams, we can perceive our lives as rich and full of promise. We can find peace and passion where once we felt despondent and devoid of hope. That's because meaning can be wrought from failure, loss, and heartache as surely as from joy.

In this, we are reminded of a journal entry by a woman who reflected on her own life and that of her friends. She wrote:

> *One question that [keeps] surfacing was how can our grown children have had such uneven paths? After reviewing all as parents we might have done wrong, I realize that maybe ultimately what we did or didn't do really didn't make the difference in their pains or successes. [This knowledge] is a kind of ultimate mystery and gives a surprising freedom.*[1]

Such freedom to move from heartache to hope is essential to shaping all our lost dreams. Without it, we can't let go our old sorrows and desires. Without it, we cling to what-might-have-been and persistent discontent. For only the free can reshape what has been lost or build what never was.

This move then from heartache to hope is full of mystery, adventure, and surprise. Nothing happening in your own world of dreams? Freely prepare for your own surprise ending.

First take heart.

Then take stock.

But above all, do take hope.

Notes

Preface

1. Hammarskjold, D. 1964, 1983. *Markings.* New York: Ballantine Books, 48.
2. de Mello, A. 1982. *The song of the bird.* Garden City, N.Y.: Image Books, Division of Doubleday & Company, Inc., 163.
3. Barnes, B. December 26?, 1989. "Waiting for Godot" author Samuel Beckett, 83, dies. *The Washington Post,* A4.
4. Chiappone, J. M. 1984. *Infertility as a non-event: Coping differences between men and women.* Ph.D. dissertation. College Park, Md.: University of Maryland.
5. Chiriboga, D. August 1991. *An historical perspective on things that never happened.* San Francisco: The American Psychological Association Annual Meeting.
6. Schlossberg, N. K., Lissitz, R., Altman, J., and Steinberg, L. 1992. *Non events: Describing a new construct.* Unpublished manuscript. College Park, Md.: University of Maryland.

Chapter 1. Non-Events: A New Name for Heartbreak?

1. Nin, A. 1967. *Diary of Anaïs Nin, volume 2: 1934–1939.* New York: The Swallow Press/Harcourt Brace & World, Inc. 89.
2. Neugarten, B. 1977. Adaptation and the life cycle. In N. K. Schlossberg and A. D. Entine (eds.), *Counseling adults,* 34–46. Monterey, Calif.: Brooks/Cole Publishing Co.
3. Ibid., 45.
4. Tavris, C. July/August 1989. Don't act your age. *American Health,* 50–58.
5. Bateson, M. C. 1989. *Composing a life.* New York: The Atlantic Monthly Press.
6. Bombeck, E. July 30, 1991. *The Washington Post,* B8.

Chapter 2. Everyone's Story

1. Keillor, G. 1985. *Lake Woebegone days.* New York: Viking Penguin Inc., 14.
2. Erikson, E., Erikson, J., and Kivnick, A. Q. 1986. *Vital involvement in old age.* New York: W. W. Norton & Co.
3. Gilligan, C. 1982. *In a different voice.* Cambridge, Mass.: Harvard University Press.
4. Campbell, J., and Moyers, B. 1988. *The power of myth.* New York: Doubleday.
5. Heilbrun, C. G. 1989. *Writing a woman's life.* New York: Ballantine.
6. Schlossberg, N. K., Lissitz, R., Altman, J., and Steinberg, L. 1992. *Non-events: Describing a new construct.* Unpublished manuscript. College Park, Md.: University of Maryland.

7. Lazarus, R. S., and Folkman, S. 1984. *Stress, approval, and coping*. New York: Springer Publishing Co.

8. DuBrim, A. October 30, 1993. Personal. *Bottom Line* in "A New Look at Job Promotions," 11.

Chapter 3. Love and Family

1. Meagher, S. 1991. *Nora*. New York: Crossroads Press.

2. Erikson, E., Erikson, J., and Kivnick, A. Q. 1986. *Vital involvement in old age*. New York: W. W. Norton & Co.

3. Weiss, R. S. 1974. The provisions of social relations. In Z. Rubin (ed.), *Doing unto others*. Englewood Cliffs, N.J.: Prentice-Hall.

4. Attractive, romantic: In search of advertisements. September 1993. *The Washingtonian*, Vol. 29, No. 4, 163.

5. Avna, J., and Waltz, D. 1992. *Celibate wives: Breaking the silence*. Los Angeles: Lowell House.

6. Rubin, L. 1985. *Just friends: The role of friendship in our lives*. New York: Harper & Row, 13.

7. Ibid., 183.

8. Hagestad, G. May 1986. Dimensions of time and family. *American Behavioral Scientist*, 689, 690, 691.

9. Planning no family, now or ever. October 1993. *American Demographics*, 23.

10. Remember, there are many ways to create a family. November 26, 1991. *The Washington Post*, Health Section.

11. Shakespeare, W. *King Lear*, Act I, Scene 4, lines 310–11.

12. Slade, M. July 25, 1991. Siblings: Growing up and closer. *The New York Times*, C1.

13. Kimmel, D. 1990. *Adulthood and aging*. New York: John Wiley & Sons, 255.

Chapter 4. The Dream of Success

1. Terkel, S. 1974. *Working*. New York: Pantheon Books, xlix.

2. Erikson, E., Erikson, J., and Kivnick, A. Q. 1986. *Vital involvement in old age*. New York: W. W. Norton & Co., 148.

3. Kilborn, P. T. September 5, 1993. A Labor Day message no one asked to hear. *The New York Times*, 1, 4.

4. Gross, J. January 9, 1992. Graduates march down aisle into job nightmare. *The New York Times*, A16.

5. Bateson, M. C. 1989. *Composing a life*. New York: The Atlantic Monthly Press, 6.

6. Intrator, N. September 1993. My security blanket. *Working Mother*.

7. Bardwick, J. M. 1986. *The plateauing trap*. New York: American Management Association, 37–38.

8. Kiechel, W., III. April 8, 1991. Overscheduled and not loving it. *Fortune*, 105.

9. Baruch, G., Barnett, R., and Rivers, C. 1983. *Life prints: New patterns of love and work for today's women*. New York & Scarborough, Ontario: New American Library.

10. Gutmann, D. C. 1977. The cross-cultural perspective: Notes toward a comparative psychology of aging. In J. E. Birren and K. W. Schaie (eds.), *Handbook of the psychology of aging* (2d. ed.). New York: Van Nostrand Reinhold Co., 7.

11. Bateson, op. cit., 9.

Chapter 5. Self and Legacy

1. Sinetar, M. 1986. *Ordinary people as monks and mystics.* New York/Mahwah: Paulist Press.
2. Terkel, S. 1974. *Working.* New York: Pantheon Books, xlix.
3. Friedan, B. 1993. *The fountain of age.* New York: Simon & Schuster, 638.
4. Labouvie-Vief, G. 1985. In J. E. Birren and K. W. Schaie (eds.), *Handbook of the psychology of aging* (2d. ed.). New York: Van Nostrand Reinhold Co., 500–30.
5. Heilbrun, C. G. 1989. *Writing a woman's life.* New York: Ballantine, 129.
6. Ibid.
7. Ryff, C. D. 1991. Possible selves in adulthood and old age: A tale of shifting horizons. *Psychology and Aging,* Vol. 6, No. 2, 286–95, 294.
8. Erikson, E., Erikson, J., and Kivnick, A. Q. 1986. *Vital involvement in old age.* New York: W. W. Norton & Co., 74–75.
9. Kimmel, D. C. 1990. *Adulthood and aging* (3d. ed.). New York: John Wiley & Sons, 16.
10. Ryff, op. cit., 285.
11. O'Farrell, N. January 4, 1994. Interview.
12. Rosenberg, M., and McCullough, B. C. 1981. Mattering: Inferred significance to parents and mental health among adolescents. In R. Simmons (ed.), *Research in community and mental health,* Vol. 2. Greenwich, Conn.: JAI Press.
13. DeBold, E., Wilson, M., and Malave, I. 1993. *Mother daughter revolution: From betrayal to power.* New York: Addison-Wesley, xv.
14. Tan, A. 1989. *The joy luck club.* New York: Putnam's.

Chapter 6. Acknowledging the Lost Dream

1. Lewis, C. S. 1956. *Till we have faces.* New York and London: Havast/H.B.J. Books/Harcourt, Brace, Jovanovich.
2. Hay, L. L. 1984. *Heal your body.* Santa Monica, Calif.: Hay House, Inc.
3. Stevens, W. 1959. The idea of order at Key West. In *Poems by Wallace Stevens.* New York: Vintage, A Division of Random House, 54.
4. B. Myerhoff Film. 1985. Rites of renewal. Owings Mills, Md.: International University Consortium and Ohio University.
5. de Mello, A. 1982. *Song of the bird.* Garden City, N.Y.: Image Books, Division of Doubleday & Company, Inc., 163.
6. Schank, R. 1990. *Tell me a story.* New York: Charles Scribner's Sons, 115.
7. Metaphors as nudges toward understanding in mental health counseling. April 1992. *Journal of Mental Health Counseling,* Vol. 14, No. 2, 234, 242.
8. Deshler, D. 1990. Fostering critical reflection in adulthood. In J. Mezerow (ed.), *Fostering critical reflection in adulthood.* San Francisco: Jossey-Bass, 296–313.

Chapter 7. Easing Your Non-Event Stress

1. Cousins, N. 1979. *Anatomy of an illness.* New York: Bantam Books, 48.
2. Lazarus, R. S. 1991. *Emotion & adaptation.* Oxford, England: Oxford University Press, 82.
3. Ibid., 122.
4. Tavris, C. 1982. *Anger: The misunderstood emotion.* New York: Simon & Schuster, A Touchstone Book, 45.

5. Hansel, J. November 1993. Discussions with therapist Jeanne Hansel.
6. Miller, S. 1985. *The shame experience.* Hillsdale, N.J.: Lawrence Erlbaum Associates.
7. Kaufman, G. 1980, 1985. *Shame: The power of caring.* Cambridge, Mass.: Schenkman Publishing Company, Inc., 127.
8. Snyder, R. 1989. Reality negotiation: From excuses to hope and beyond. *Journal of Social and Clinical Psychology,* Vol. 8, No. 2, 130–57.
9. Lazarus, op. cit., 247–48.
10. Tavris, op. cit., 226.
11. Lazarus, op. cit., 247–48.
12. Heiser, L. May 1992. Analysis of coping strategies used by those experiencing non-events. Typed paper for EDCP 606, University of Maryland, College Park.
13. Doka, K. J. 1989. *Disenfranchised grief.* New York: Lexington Books, 4.
14. Ibid.
15. Kushner, H. S. 1989. *Who needs God.* New York: Summit Books, 18.
16. Therapists see religion as aid, not illusion. September 1991. *The New York Times,* C1.
17. Siegel, B. 1986. *Love, medicine, and miracles.* New York: Harper & Row, 144.
18. Cousins, op. cit., 39.

Chapter 8. Shifting the Focus to Hope

1. Dickinson, E. 1962. Hope is the thing with feathers. In O. Williams (ed.), *The Mentor book of major American poets.* New American Library, 187.
2. Bridges, W. 1980. *Transitions: Making sense of life's changes.* New York: Addison-Wesley Publishing Co., 17.
3. Ibid., 90.
4. Ibid., 114.
5. Ebaugh, H. R. F. 1988. *Becoming an ex: The process of role exit.* Chicago: University of Chicago Press, 23.
6. Viorst, J. 1986. *Necessary losses.* New York: Simon & Schuster.
7. Taylor, S. E. 1989. *Positive illusions.* New York: Basic Books, Inc., xi.
8. Yalom, I. D. 1989. *Love's executioner.* New York: Basic Books, Inc., 154.
9. Seligman, M. E. P. 1991. *Learned optimism.* New York: Alfred A. Knopf, 218.
10. Rites and independence: New ceremonies for new people. November 1984. *Ms.*

Chapter 9. Reshaping the Dream

1. Deng Ming-Dao. 1992. *365 tao daily meditations.* San Francisco: Harper San Francisco, A Division of Harper Collins Publications, 1.
2. Neugarten, B. 1977. Adaptation and the life cycle. In N. K. Schlossberg and A. D. Entine (eds.), *Counseling adults.* Monterey, Calif.: Brooks/Cole Publishing Co.
3. Schlossberg, N. K. 1994. *Overwhelmed: Coping with life's ups and downs.* New York: Macmillan, Lexington Books.
4. Lazarus, R., and Folkman, S. 1984. *Stress, appraisal, and coping.* New York: Springer Publishing Co.
5. Steinem, G. 1992. *Revolution from within: A book of self-esteem.* New York: Vanity Fair, 91.

Afterword: From Heartache to Hope

1. Rowe, A. L. 1992. Unpublished letter sent to friends and acquaintances.

Index

A

acknowledgment of non-events, 52, 137–50
  examples of, 138–41
  making meaning in, 142–50
  metaphors and, 52, 148–50
  naming and, 52, 144–46
  public vs. private non-events and, 142
  strategies in, 52
  telling your story and, 52, 146–48
acupuncture, 178
ADD (Attention Deficit Disorder), 119
adoption, 20, 33–34, 146
ads, "ISO," 62
Adult Children of Alcoholics, 175
African Americans, 61, 82
age:
  femininity and masculinity and, 105
  intellectual plasticity and, 119
  need to matter and, 126, 130–32
  need to transfer and, 126–30
  self-image and, 123–24
  sense of integrity and, 121
  transitions and, 29, 31–32

agency, 163
"age of anxiety," 156
AIDS, 132
Alcoholics Anonymous, 104, 175
American Demographics, 71
anger, 66, 92, 152, 153, 155–56, 163
anxiety, 153, 156–57
apathy, 154, 160–61
appearance, physical, 42, 117–18
assumptions, necessity of, 195
attachment, 59
Attention Deficit Disorder (ADD), 119
Auden, W. H., 156
Augustine, Saint, 122
aural learning, 118
Avna, Joan, 66

B

baby boomers, 123
Bar and Bat Mitzvahs, 200
Bardwick, Judith, 96, 99
Bateson, Mary Catherine, 32, 91, 109
"Beast in the Jungle, The" (James), 19
beauty, standards of, 42, 117–18

Beckett, Samuel, 19
best friends, 68
betrayal, 58
biological clocks, 28–29, 119
blame, 166–67
"blessed rage for order," 143
bliss, following of, 40
body-mind connection, 196
Bombeck, Erma, 32–33
borderline emotions, 153
breast cancer, 196
breathing, deep, 178
Bridges, William, 182, 183,
     185–86
broken dreams, *see* non-events
Buddhism, 121, 175, 194

C

Campbell, Joseph, 40
cancer, 161–62, 196
"Candid Camera," 177
careers, career non-events, 20, 38,
     39, 47, 49, 87–111, 140
   competence and, 89–90
   coping strategies for, 214–16
   elusive success and, 92–96
   issues in, 40
   job loss and, 197–98
   making meaning and, 143
   and meaning of success, 109–11
   plateauing and, 96–101
   and reassurance of worth, 62
   retirement and, 51, 90, 101–2,
        131, 183
   shifting of focus and, 192–93
   transformed assumptions and,
        90–92
   women and, 40–41, 103–9
Catholicism, 206
Celibate Wives (Avna and Waltz), 66

children:
   adoption of, 20, 33–34, 146
   cultural and political legacies
        and, 133–34
   death of, 67
   leaving home by, 42–43
   of older parents, 74–75
   parents' expectations of, 42,
        78–79, 195–96
   parents seen as omnipotent by,
        194
   religious upbringing of, 65–66
   sibling relationships between,
        80–81
   stories and, 146–48
clocks:
   biological, 28–29, 119
   social, 29–31, 60
closure, 21, 132
coconut parable, 18
coming-of-age rituals, 200
compassion, 154
competence, sense of, 40, 89–90,
     95–96, 103
Composing a Life (Bateson), 32, 91
Confession, 206
content plateauing, 99–101
control, 20, 46, 48–49, 53, 84
coping strategies, 213–16
   emotion-focused, 214, 215–16
   problem-focused, 214–15
Cousins, Norman, 151, 177
cultural and political legacies,
     133–34
cultural norms, 30

D

daydreaming, taking steps after, 138
death of a child, 67
deep breathing, 178

delayed dreams, 69–70

delayed non-events, 45, 189, 193–94

de Mello, Anthony, 18, 146

Deng Ming-Dao, 205

depression, 92, 160, 163

Deshler, David, 149, 150

desire, as source of suffering, 121

despair, 21, 33, 35, 58, 121, 209–11

developmental stages, 29, 31–32, 39–40, 89

Dickinson, Emily, 181

diets, addiction to, 117

discontinuity, 193

disenfranchised grief, 169–70

disgust, 153

disputation, 199

divorce, 68, 217
  naming and, 144, 145–46

doing:
  identity through, 115
  learning by, 118

Doka, Kenneth J., 169

dream analysis theory, 148

dream paths, 207–12

dream reshaping, 20, 36, 38, 54, 85, 99, 135–221
  acknowledgment and, 52, 137–50
  components of, 50–53
  dreaming the new and possible, 216–17
  dream paths and, 207–12
  easing of non-event stress, 52, 151–79
  seeds of transformation and, 212–21
  shifting focus to hope, 181–203
  situation assessment and, 218–21
  strategies in, 213–16
  support and, 217

dreams, 40–44
  broken, see non-events
  delayed, 69–70
  grief after fulfillment of, 170–71
  importance of, 36
  interconnectedness of, 39
  letting go of, 49, 53
  Nin on, 25
  parental, 42
  reclamation of, 21, 33–34
  "too big," 38
  triggers and, 38, 44, 53–54, 107

DuBrim, Andrew J., 49

dyslexia, 119

E

easing non-event stress, 151–79
  emotions as signals in, 153–63
  through faith, 52, 174–76
  grief and, 52, 167–71
  through humor, 52, 176–77
  through journal writing, 52, 173–74
  labels and, 163–67
  other means of, 171–78
  seeking support for, 52, 171–73
  way stations and, 179

Ebaugh, Helen Rose Fuchs, 187, 188

education, 38, 47, 48, 70
  issues in, 40

egocentricity of teenagers, 37, 38

emotional isolation, 58–59

emotion-focused coping strategies, 214, 215–16

emotions, 38
  borderline, 153
  goals and, 153
  labeling of, 163–67
  as signals, 153–63

envy, 153, 161

Erikson, Erik, 31, 39–40, 58, 84–85, 89, 95, 121, 125
exiting, process of, 101–2, 182–89
expectations, letting go of, 53, 194–96

F

failure, importance of, 32–33
faith, 52, 174–76
families, family non-events, 38, 39, 58–60, 68–85
   delayed dreams and, 69–70
   essential points about, 84–85
   infertility and, 70–73, 75–76
   late parenthood and, 74–75
   miscarriage and, 73–74
   missing members and, 76–77
   transformations and, 68–69
   women's careers and, 40–41, 103–9
   see also children; parents
feminine qualities in men, 105
fertility treatment, 75
fidelity, 39, 40
firing, 197–98
fluidity, 32
Folkman, Susan, 49, 213–14
Fortune, 100
Foster Care Youth United (National Public Radio publication), 148
Fountain of Age, The (Friedan), 116
Freud, Sigmund, 148
Friedan, Betty, 116, 117
friends, 217
   marriage relationships and, 58–59
   sense of timing influenced by, 30–31
   social, 68
   transitions aided by, 66–68
   types of, 68
   see also relationships
fright, 153
Frost, Robert, 148
"fruit pickers" metaphor, 149–50
Funt, Allen, 177

G

gay men, 69, 78, 81–82
generativity, self-absorption vs., 125–26
gerontology, 119
Gilligan, Carol, 39
goals, as source of emotional signals, 153
God, 19, 122, 175
grief, 36, 52, 73, 167–71
   disenfranchised, 169–70
   expressing emotions of, 170
   after fulfillment of dreams, 170–71
   process of, 167–69
guidance, obtaining, 59
guilt, 89, 152, 153, 157–58, 162
Gutmann, David, 105

H

Hagestad, Gunhild, 69
Hammarskjold, Dag, 17
hangover identities, 188
happiness, 154
Hay, Louise L., 139
health insurance, 82
Heal Your Body (Hay), 139
Heilbrun, Carolyn, 40, 123–24
helplessness, perception of, 152–53
high-hope individuals, low-hope individuals vs., 163
homosexuality, 69, 78, 81–82, 191

hope, 20, 22, 85, 154
  as basic human strength, 39
  coping strategies and, 214–16
  Dickinson on, 181
  easing non-event stress through,
    162–63
  exiting and, 182–89
  holding vs. letting go of, 207–9
  hopelessness vs., 46–47
  moving from heartache to,
    223–25
  operational components of, 163
  through reclamation of dreams,
    33–34
  refocusing and, 194–203
  reframing and, 198–200
  shifting the focus to, 181–203
  varieties of non-events and,
    189–94
"Hope Scale," 163
humor, 52, 176–77, 202

I

idealized self-image, 123–24
identity:
  doing as source of, 115
  hangover, 188
illness:
  and acknowledgment of non-
    events, 138–40
  need to matter and, 126, 130–32
  need to transfer and, 126–30
  see also easing non-event stress
illusions, facing of, 53, 196–98
industry, inferiority vs., 89
infertility, 20, 60, 70–73, 75–76,
    199–200
  secondary, 27, 72–73
inner peace, 120–22
insurance, health, 82

integration, social, 59, 60
integrity, sense of, 121
intellectual capacity, 118–20
intellectual plasticity, 119
intelligence, types of, 118
interdependence, separation vs., 39
intimacy, 58, 72, 104
invisibility, feelings of, 123
Islam, 206
isolation, social vs. emotional,
    58–59
"ISOs" (In Search Of ads), 62
"Is That All There Is?," 122

J

James, Henry, 19
jealousy, 153, 161
Jesus, 194
jobs, *see* careers
journal writing, 52, 173–74
Joy Luck Club, The (Tan), 134
Judaism, 206
Jung, Carl, 148
Just Friends (Rubin), 66

K

Kaufman, Gershen, 157–58
Keillor, Garrison, 37, 38
Kierkegaard, Søren, 162
Kilborn, Peter, 90
Kimmel, Douglas, 82, 126
kinesthetic learning, 118
King Lear (Shakespeare), 78
Kushner, Harold, 174

L

labeling, 163–67
  see also naming
laughter, physical effects of,
    176–77

Lazarus, Richard, 49, 153, 164, 168, 213–14
learning, modes of, 118
learning disabilities, 119, 215
legacy, definition of, 127
legacy non-events, 40, 125–34
    cultural and political, 133–34
    generativity and, 125–26
    importance of, 134
    need to matter and, 126, 130–32
    need to transfer and, 126–30
lesbians, 69, 78, 81–82, 191
"Let Me Come In," 114
Lewis, C. S., 137
life:
    fluidity vs. linearity of, 32
    sensed as meaningless, 38
limbo, 185–87
linearity, 32, 39–40
literature, non-events described in, 19
loneliness, social vs. emotional, 58–59
Long Day's Journey into Night (O'Neill), 166–67
love, 39, 40, 60–66, 154
    missed opportunities and, 65–66
    searching for, 62–64
    sense of completion and, 64–65
    unconditional, 77
Love's Executioner (Yalom), 197
low-hope individuals, high-hope individuals vs., 163

M
"malignant" tendencies, 89
"man with new direction," 144
marriage, 140–41
    friendships compared with, 58–59
    homosexuals and, 82
    race and, 61
    sexless, 66, 84
    see also divorce; relationships
Marx Brothers, 177
Maryland, University of, at College Park, 19–20
masculine qualities in women, 105
massage, 178
maturity, 39
Meagher, Sandra, 57
meaning, making, 142–50
    naming as means of, 144–46
    using metaphors in, 146–48
meaninglessness of life, sense of, 38
meditation, 178
men, feminine qualities in, 105
Me Nobody Knows, The (Friedman and Holt), 114
metaphors, 52, 148–50
Miller, Susan, 157
mind-body connection, 196
miscarriage, 73–74
misfortune, response to, 18
modes of learning, 118
Mother Daughter Revolution (DeBold, Wilson and Malave), 133
Ms., 202
myths:
    definition of, 40
    as source of dreams, 40–41
    women and, 210

N
naming, 52, 144–46
    see also labeling
National Public Radio, 148
Native American vision quests, 200
Necessary Losses (Viorst), 195–96
Neugarten, Bernice, 28–29, 212

neutral zones, 185–86
New Age, 122
New Year's resolutions, 206
New York Times, 80, 175
Nin, Anaïs, 25
non-events:
    acknowledgment of, 137–50
    definition and examples of,
        18–22, 26–28, 35–36
    delayed, 189, 193–94
    evaluation of, 164–66
    failure and, 32–33
    four varieties of, 189–94
    gauging impact of, 45–50
    in literature, 19
    of other people, 34–35, 45, 54
    personal, 189–90
    as positive, negative, or neutral,
        46, 49–50, 54
    probability as essential to, 28
    public vs. private, 142
    range of issues related to, 38–40,
        53
    reactions to, 20
    research on, 19–20
    resultant, 189, 192–93
    ripple, 189
    as source of despair, 21
    sudden vs. gradual, 20, 46,
        47–48, 54
    timing and, 28–31, 35, 53, 60
    types of, 38, 44–45
    understanding of, 37–54
norms, cultural, 30
nurturance, 59, 60, 95, 104

O
obtaining guidance, 59
O'Farrell, Neil, 128–29, 131–32
"off-time," 29

"Old Maidhood," 202
O'Neill, Eugene, 166–67, 187
other people, non-events of, 34–35,
    45, 54

P
parenthood, late, 74–75
parents:
    emotional separation from,
        43–44
    expectations of, 42, 78–79,
        195–96
    non-events of, 34–35
    seen as omnipotent, 194
parties, 176
pathways, 163
personal ads, 62
personal non-events, 189–90
physical appearance, 42, 117–18
plasticity, intellectual, 119
plateauing, 96–101
    content, 99–101
    structural, 96–99
poetry, 148
political and cultural legacies,
    133–34
Positive Illusions (Taylor), 196
prayer, 175–76
pride, 154
private non-events, public non-
        events vs., 142
probability, possibility vs., 28
problem-focused coping strategies,
        214–15
Psalms, 194
psychologists, 156
psychotherapy, 36, 148
public non-events, private non-
        events vs., 142
purpose, sense of, 40

Q

"quiet desperation," 21

R

race, 82
    marriage and, 61
Ramadan, 206
reassurance of worth, 59, 60, 61, 62,
    81
refocusing, 194–203
    definition and strategies for,
      52–53
    facing of illusions, 196–98
    letting go of expectations and,
      194–96
    reframing and, 198–200
    in religious teachings, 194
    rites of passage and, 200–203
reframing, 53, 198–200
regret, 159
relationships, 20, 38, 58
    issues in, 40
    love and, 60–66
    needs met by, 59
    single people and, 60–64
    see also friends; marriage
relaxation techniques, 178
reliable alliance, sense of, 59
relief, 154, 161–62
    see also easing non-event stress
religion, 36, 65, 121
    children's upbringing and, 65–66
    refocusing in, 194
    resolutions in, 206
    rites of passage in, 200
    see also spirituality
reproach, 114–17
reshaping, *see* dream reshaping
resolutions, 206
resultant non-events, 189, 192–93

retirement, 51, 90, 101–2, 131, 183
Rich, Adrienne, 123
ripple non-events, 189, 190–92
rites of passage, 53, 200–203
"Rites of Renewal," 144
rituals, 53, 80, 202
role exit process, 187–88
Rosenberg, Morris, 131
Rubin, Lillian, 66
Ryff, Carol, 124, 126–27

S

Sacrament of Reconciliation, 206
sadness, 153, 160
Schank, Roger, 147
secondary infertility, 27, 72–73
self-absorption, generativity vs.,
    125–26
self-assessment system, 213
self-censure, 114–17
self-evaluative horizons, 124
self-image, idealized, 123–24
self-improvement, 20
self non-events, 113–24
    idealized self-image and,
      123–24
    importance of, 134
    inner peace and, 120–22
    intellectual capacity and,
      118–20
    issues in, 40, 114–24
    physical appearance and, 42,
      117–18
    reproach and, 66, 114–17
    societal non-events vs., 40–42,
      44
    spirituality and, 122–23
self-reproach, 66, 114–17
Seligman, Martin, 199–200
separation, interdependence vs., 39

75 percent rule, 209
sexless marriages, 66, 84
sex roles, 42, 106–7
sexual appeal, women's span of, 60
Shakespeare, William, 78
shame, 66, 152, 153, 157–58
Shame: The Power of Caring (Kaufman),
    157–58
Shirley Valentine (Russell), 65
shoulds, 114
Siegel, Bernie, 176–77
Sills, Beverly, 102
Sinetar, Marsha, 113
singlehood, celebration of, 202
single people, 60–64, 202
situation assessment, 218–21
Snyder, Rick, 162–63
social clocks, 29–31, 60
social friends, 68
social integration, 59, 60
social isolation, 58–59
societal non-events, 40–42, 44
Song of the Bird, The (de Mello), 18
spirituality, 36, 38
    easing non-event stress through,
        174–76
    self non-events and, 122–23
    see also religion
stages, developmental, 29, 31–32,
    39–40, 89
Steinem, Gloria, 216
Stevens, Wallace, 143
stories, telling of, 52, 146–48
stress, *see* easing non-event stress
stress-reduction techniques, 177–78
structural plateauing, 96–99
suffering, desire as source of, 121
support, seeking of, 52, 171–73,
    217
survivor's guilt, 162

T

Tan, Amy, 134
Tavris, Carol, 31–32, 155, 167
Taylor, Shelley E., 196, 197
teenage egocentricity, 37, 38
telling your story, 52, 146–48
Tell Me a Story (Schank), 147
Terkel, Studs, 87, 113
therapy, 36
Thoreau, Henry David, 21
timing, non-events and, 28–31, 35,
    53, 60
transfer, need to, 126–30
transitions:
    age and, 29, 31–32
    evaluation of, 49–50
    friends and, 66–68
    importance of, 29
    phases of, 182–83
triggers, 38, 44, 53–54, 107
trust, 39, 40
truth, metaphors and, 148–50

U

unambiguous women, 40–41
unconditional love, 77
unemployment, guilt and, 157

V

"vacations" from life, 186
Viorst, Judith, 195–96
vision quests, 200
visual learning, 118
Vital Involvement in Old Age (Erikson,
    Erikson and Kivnick), 125

W

Waiting for Godot (Beckett), 19
Wall Street, 110
Waltz, Diana, 66

way stations, 179
Weiss, Robert, 58–59, 84–85
Woman of Distinction awards, 32
"woman with options," 144
women:
    career vs. family issues and,
        40–41, 103–9
    critical underlying concerns of
        men and, 39
    cultural myths about, 210
    feelings of invisibility and, 123
    masculine qualities in, 105
    span of sexual appeal of, 60
    unambiguous, 40–41

work:
    friends at, 68
    see also careers, career non-events
Working (Terkel), 87, 113
Working Mother, 93–94
worth, reassurance of, 59, 60, 61, 62,
    81
writing, journal, 52, 173–74

Y

Yalom, Irvin, 197
yoga, 178
Yom Kippur, 206